THE FACTS ABOUT
CHILD PHYSICAL ABUSE

TITLES IN THE FACTS ABOUT ... SERIES

THE FACTS ABOUT
CHILD
PHYSICAL ABUSE

BILL GILLHAM

CASSELL

Cassell
Villiers House
41/47 Strand
London WC2N 5JE

387 Park Avenue South
New York
NY 10016–8810

Copyright © Bill Gillham 1994

First published 1994

British Library Cataloguing-in-Publication Data
A catalogue record for this book is available from the British Library.

ISBN: 0–304–32665–8 (hardback)
0–304–32663–1 (paperback)

Typeset by Fakenham Photosetting Limited, Fakenham, Norfolk
Printed and bound in Great Britain by Biddles Ltd, Guildford and King's Lynn

CONTENTS

Contents

SERIES FOREWORD

The idea for this series came from an awareness that much of the media hype, and some of the professional practice, relating to major social problems involving children and adolescents was singularly ill-informed. At the same time there was a notable lack of short, accessible summaries of the relevant research data by which people could inform themselves.

Not surprisingly, the conclusions that are drawn from a careful consideration of the evidence challenge many generally held assumptions – at all levels of popular and professional concern.

Bill Gillham

ACKNOWLEDGEMENTS

Acknowledgement is gratefully given to Anne Toland who word-processed and checked the manuscript, to Judith Gillham for editorial help at the stage of re-writing, and to Gill Morris of Strathclyde University's Andersonian Library for expert advice and help in carrying out on-line searches. Many points in the evidence were discussed with Gary Tanner, who also assisted in the preparation of some figures. The following authors and publishers have kindly given permission to reproduce or derive from copyright figures and tables: The Department of Health for Figure 3.1 and Tables 3.1 and 3.2; S. J. Creighton and the NSPCC for Figures 3.3, 3.4, 3.5, 3.6, 5.1 and 5.4 and Tables 3.3, 3.4, 3.5, 5.3 and 5.4; J. A. Rosenthal and Pergamon Press for Figure 3.7; the Office of Population Censuses and Surveys and the Controller of HMSO for Figures 4.1, 4.2, 4.9 and 4.10 and Tables 3.6, 3.7 and 4.1; A. B. Russell, C. M. Trainor and the American Humane Association for Tables 3.8, 3.9 and 5.1; A. L. Wilson and the South Dakota State Medical Association for Figure 4.3 and Table 4.2; the Registrar General Scotland for Figure 4.4; J. Jason, M. M. Carpenter, C. W. Tyler and the American Public Health Association for Figures 4.5 and 4.6; J. D. Alfaro and Charles C. Thomas Inc. for Table 4.3; J. Jason, N. D. Andereck and Pergamon Press for Figure 4.7; R. Anderson, R. Ambrosino, D. Valentine, M. Lauderdale and Pergamon Press for Figure 4.8; C. J. Hobbs, J. M. Wynne and The British Medical Association for Figure 5.2 and Table 5.2; J. Jason, S. L. Williams, A. Burton, R. Rochat and the American Medical Association for Figure 5.3; A. W. Baker, S. P. Duncan and Pergamon Press for Table 5.5; A. M. Cotterill and Pergamon Press for Figure 6.1; J. Kaufman, E. Zigler and John Wiley for Table 6.1; P. M. Crittenden, The Association for Child Psychology and Psychiatry and Pergamon Press for Table 7.1; M. Rutter and The American Orthopsychiatric Association Inc. for Figure 7.1.

1

AN HISTORICAL
PERSPECTIVE

It is easy for us to accept that in periods of history and cultures remote from our own the maltreatment of children was commonplace, and often sanctioned by law and custom. Summarizing the history of child abuse and infanticide Radbill (1968) writes:

> Throughout history there are accounts of the customary extremes in the chastisement of children. Pepys beat his boy until he (Pepys) was out of breath; John Wesley, Frederick the Great, Lady Jane Grey, and many others in adult life complained bitterly of their treatment in childhood. *It always was taken for granted that the parents and guardians of children had every right to treat their children as they saw fit.* (p. 4, emphasis added)

The last sentence in this quotation is emphasized because it has remained a persistent barrier to the improvement of child treatment. The boundaries have been pushed back, and are more clearly defined in some areas, but they remain.

Radbill comments that:

> No parent now has the right to kill his child, and there is no distinction between infanticide and murder. The legal limits to chastisement of children, however, are not clearcut; such limitations have to be supplemented by public opinion. (p. 6)

1

As public opinion changes so do our criteria for, and acceptance of, child abuse.

The most striking thing about the history of childhood and child maltreatment is how recently the grossest forms of abuse were permitted; and how slowly public opinion and action were mobilized. It is not a matter of remote history; in some respects, as we shall see, it is a matter of contemporary history.

Pinchbeck and Hewitt (1973) in their historical review, *Children in English Society*, write that:

> until late in the nineteenth century, both Parliament
> and the national press were largely unconcerned with
> the way in which parents treated their children,
> regarding even the most barbarous cruelty as beyond
> comment and beyond public intervention since
> children were not then regarded as citizens in their
> own right. (p. 611)

Remarkable also is the degree to which the 'private' maltreatment of children was matched by public maltreatment, as part of the process of law. Again we do not have to dig into ancient history:

> Up to 1780, the penalty for over two hundred offences
> was death by hanging, and many a child, like the little
> girl of seven hanged in the market place at Norwich for
> stealing a petticoat, was hanged for a trivial offence
> which in our own day would normally entail a
> probation order. Children were among those publicly
> hanged after the Gordon Riots. 'I never saw boys cry so
> much,' commented George Selwyn, who witnessed the
> execution of some of these miserable children. There
> are, in fact, instances of children younger than seven
> being executed, as, for example, the pitiable case of a
> child of six who cried for his mother on the scaffold. On
> one day alone, in February 1814, at the Old Bailey

Sessions, five children were condemned to death;
Fowler, aged twelve, and Wolfe, aged twelve, for
burglary in a dwelling; Morris, aged eight, Solomons,
aged nine, and Burrell, aged eleven, for burglary and
stealing a pair of shoes. (Pinchbeck and Hewitt, *op. cit.*,
pp. 351–2)

In the mid-nineteenth century concern for children focused
mainly on public manifestations of maltreatment – employment in
mines, factories and the like. The use of small boys to climb inside
chimney flues was sentimentalized in Charles Kingsley's 1863
classic *The Water Babies*. But it was not until 1874 that the use of
boys for sweeping chimneys was prohibited by Act of Parliament.

Property rather than *persons* was the priority in law. Until 1814 it
was not an offence, under English law, to steal a child (no value)
unless he were clothed; in which case the person taking the child
could be convicted of stealing its clothes (Pinchbeck and Hewitt,
op. cit., p. 360). To be a child was, necessarily, to be at risk.

'In ancient times,' writes Radbill, 'infancy was a dangerous time
of life' (p. 6). It remained so until late in the nineteenth century
and, as can be seen in Chapter 3, is still the main 'at risk' age for
physical abuse. It was concern over the high rates of infanticide
that prompted the first public interventions into the private care of
children, in particular the activities of the so-called 'baby farm-
ers': women who fostered babies for gain and took the simplest
solution to reduce their expenses.

The number of babies found abandoned, both dead and alive,
in the major cities of the US and the UK led to concerted action in
the 1860s and 1870s. The New York Foundling Hospital, a grim
Victorian pile, was established on Randall's Island in 1869. By the
year 1873, no fewer than 1,392 foundlings were left there. Radbill
(*op. cit.*) cites the New York Medical Register of the same year as
reporting that 122 infants were found dead in the city's streets,
alleyways and rivers.

An identical situation existed in London and was projected into

3

public awareness by the exposure of a particularly sensational case of 'baby farming'. Pinchbeck and Hewitt comment:

> As in so many other fields of social reform, concerted action was impossible in the absence of convincing information, and even when such information had been collected, some particularly sensational piece of evidence was often needed to rally a wavering public to the cause of the reformers. An instance of this was the way the Infant Life Protection Act found its way on to the Statute Book. About the beginning of May in the year 1870 the bodies of sixteen young babies were found in Brixton and Peckham, some in the streets and some in open spaces. It was not unusual to find dead babies in such places in London at that time. In 1870 the number so found was no less than 276, the majority being under one week old. (*op. cit.*, pp. 612–13)

They go on to describe a process of detection which ranks with the most lurid forms of Victorian fiction. An important result for child care in the UK was the formation of the Infant Life Protection Society which led directly to the Infant Life Protection Act of 1872. Although a landmark piece of legislation it still did not stop the worst practices (the killing of unwanted babies by women who had taken them into care). The Act was amended in 1887 following the execution of a notorious baby farmer, Mrs Dyer, the year before.

The more general problem of the cruelty and neglect of children was dealt with even more slowly and, it has to be said, not without elements of comic irony.

In the US the first challenge to parental rights came about in New York in 1874 (Fontana, 1971), and was brought to litigation by the Society for the Prevention of Cruelty to Animals. Mary Ellen, a child who had been starved and brutally beaten by her adoptive parents was successfully removed from her home on the basis that a child, as a member of the animal kingdom '. . . was entitled to at least the same justice as a common cur on the streets' (Fontana, *op. cit.*, p. 185).

The publicity surrounding this case led to the establishment of the first American society concerned with child protection – the New York Society for the Prevention of Cruelty to Children; other cities soon followed New York's example.

In 1881 Thomas Agnew, a Liverpool merchant and banker, visited the United States and saw at first hand the progress that was being made there. Returning to England the following year he discussed the experiments he had seen with his MP, Samuel Smith.

Pinchbeck and Hewitt (*op. cit.*) write:

> The result of the member's support was that a few
> weeks later, at a meeting organised by the Society for
> the Prevention of Cruelty to Animals, an appeal for a
> Dog's Home became extended into an appeal for the
> protection of children. That societies to protect animals
> from cruelty were established before societies to
> protect children is one of the better known, bizarre
> features of English social history [and, as we have seen
> above, of American social history as well!]. Less well
> known, perhaps, is that Parliament itself intervened to
> protect animals from abuse more than three-quarters
> of a century before it thought it proper to extend
> statutory protection to the young child. As in the case
> of infant life protection, so here, reluctance to legislate
> was rooted in the contemporary view that it was both
> improper and, indeed, unsafe to invade the privacy of
> the home. (pp. 621–2)

The Liverpool Society for the Prevention of Cruelty to Children was founded in 1883; others were established in Bristol and Birmingham in the same year. London, Glasgow and Hull followed suit two years later.

By 1889, thirty-one cities and towns had formed similar organizations and in that year the London society amalgamated with some of those in the provinces to form the National Society for the Prevention of Cruelty to Children, by which name it is still known. Note that this is little more than a hundred years ago, only just outside living memory. Benjamin Waugh, a Congregational Minister of dynamic character, was honorary secretary of the Society and proved instrumental in urging through Parliament, in that same year, a bill to protect children from cruelty by their parents. The information garnered by the various Societies mobilized public opinion and focused the need for legislation.

Post-legislation the reports of the NSPCC on the details of cruelty to children served to maintain the matter in public consciousness. Tuckwell (1894, cited in Pinchbeck and Hewitt) gives the following quotation from the NSPCC's official journal describing cases met by the Society's officers:

> Punishing a child by putting pins into its nostrils;
> putting lighted matches up them; biting a child's wrist
> until a wound was made, and then burning the wound
> with lighted matches; burning the hands of a boy of six
> with matches; biting them till they bled the limbs of a
> seven months old baby; forcing the bone ring of a
> feeding bottle up and down the throat of a three
> months old baby till it bled; throwing a little girl of two
> years, ill with bronchitis, out of its bedroom window,
> breaking its bones and ending its life; ... leaving a
> baby unlifted out of its cradle for weeks, till toadstools
> grew around the child out of its own rottenness; ...
> keeping the stumps of little amputated legs sore, to
> have the child with its little face puckered up in pain, to
> excite pity; tying a rope round a boy of six, dipping
> him in the canal, leaving him immersed till exhausted,
> bringing him up, recovering him, and putting him in
> again, repeating misery time after time; ... keeping a

child always in a cool cellar till its flesh became green
... (pp. 132–3)

Between 1889 and 1894, almost six thousand people were prosecuted under the Prevention of Cruelty to Children Act, the great majority of whom were convicted. Many more cases were investigated.

The Act was revised in 1894 and the following year the Society was incorporated by Royal Charter, an imprimatur of great importance at that time.

One limitation of the Act, however, was that it dealt only with wilful cruelty. Neglect was another matter. Before 1870 little was known about the physical condition of the nation's children in any systematic fashion. The new 'Board Schools' established by the Education Acts of 1870 and 1876 brought to middle-class attention the whole range of children from the poorer classes. Pinchbeck and Hewitt (*op. cit.*) comment:

> Now, for the first time, could be seen, *en masse*, the
> results of the urbanisation of England expressed in
> terms of child health, physical and mental ... Between
> 1889 and 1906, five investigations were made into the
> physical condition of schoolchildren in London. All
> revealed the same disturbing facts of stunted growth,
> weakly bodies, and chronic malnutrition. (pp. 632–3)

This mounting concern was increased by a report made in 1902 by the Inspector General of Recruiting on the reasons for rejecting recruits for the Boer War. A large proportion had proved quite unfit for military service. The implications of this for the practice of child health were immediately recognized, and tackled with typical Victorian vigour. The provision of school meals and the extension of school medical services were only part of the response. In 1908 a comprehensive Children's Act was passed which sought to give children social rights independent of their

parents; something that would have been unthinkable a genera-
tion earlier. During the debate on the Bill the Lord Advocate
declared that:

> There was a time in the history of this House when a Bill
> of this kind would have been treated as a most
> revolutionary measure; and, half a century ago, if such
> a measure had been introduced it would have been
> said that the British Constitution was being
> undermined. Now a Bill of this kind finds itself in
> smooth water from the outset. This measure is not the
> development of the political ideas of one party, but the
> gradual development of a quickened sense on the part
> of the community at large of the duty it owes to the
> Children. (Hansard, 1908, cited by Pinchbeck and
> Hewitt)

The Children's Act became known as the 'Children's Charter'
and was certainly a remarkable piece of legislation for that time.
The pattern of child care and protection it established was to
remain in place for almost half a century. It was a period of key
legislation that appeared definitive (the 1913 Mental Health Act is
another example). If problems were not entirely solved they were
at least recognized and managed. That half-century has been
called the 'silent period' of child care. The energy of late Victorian
reformers and politicians had set up institutions as solid as their
buildings, the limitations of which only slowly became apparent.

Writing in the mid-1960s, Radbill (*op. cit.*) comments:

> Abuse of children has excited periodic waves of
> sympathy, each rising to a high pitch, and then
> curiously subsiding until the next period of excitation.
> We owe the present wave of excitation to the relatively
> new discipline of pediatric radiology. (p. 18)

A new phase in the history of child protection was ushered in by
a paper describing the 'battered child syndrome'.

THE 'BATTERED CHILD SYNDROME'

In 1962 Dr Henry Kempe and his associates at the University of Colorado School of Medicine published a paper entitled 'The battered child syndrome' in the *Journal of the American Medical Association* (Kempe *et al.*, 1962).

This paper, describing a condition of 'unrecognized trauma' in young children marked the beginning of a new era in child protection. Detailing the signs of serious physical abuse, the authors comment in their introduction that: 'Unfortunately, it is frequently not recognized or, if diagnosed, is inadequately handled by the physician because of hesitation to bring the case to the attention of the proper authorities' (p. 17).

The scale and speed of the popular and professional response to this paper were remarkable, particularly in the US where Gelardo and Sanford (1987) report that:

> In 1963 alone, 18 bills to protect the victims of child
> abuse were introduced in the US Congress and 11 of
> them were passed that year. Mandatory child abuse
> reporting laws were instituted in all 50 states by 1965.
> (p. 138)

In the UK the response was somewhat slower but essentially similar procedures were established by the late sixties, embodied in the 1968 Children and Young Persons Act. The detail of this response and of the establishment of professional child protection agencies is the subject of a later chapter. What has to be considered here is why, for so long, such a large-scale problem of severe physical abuse was obscured and rarely recognized for what it was.

The evidence was there in the professional literature, even if overlaid with qualifications or deflected by a search for explanations other than the 'obvious' ones. Reading the research literature prior to the publication of Kempe's paper, one can see the problem gradually assuming the form that we now recognize.

There are many lessons to be learnt from a careful scrutiny of the process of discovery of an unsuspected problem: in particular that it requires a shift of perception, a reformulation of our established ideas. In the field of child abuse it is as much an intellectual as a clinical discovery.

In 1946 Dr John Caffey, a radiologist based in New York, published a paper in the *American Journal of Roentgenology* (UK readers will be more familiar with the term 'radiology'), where he described cases of multiple fractures in the long bones of infants suffering from subdural hematoma (bleeding underneath the intracranial covering of the brain). He had been collecting these cases for a period of some twenty years. In his discussion Caffey points out that although it is generally accepted in the clinical literature that subdural hematoma is due to trauma, 'a history of injury is lacking in almost one-half of cases' (p. 172).

He continues:

> The negative history of trauma in so many cases can
> probably be best explained by assuming that
> sometimes lay observers do not properly evaluate
> ordinary but causally significant accidents especially
> falls on the head, and that other important traumatic
> episodes pass unnoticed or are forgotten by the time
> delayed cranial symptoms appear ...
>
> The absence of trauma to the fractured bones cannot
> be explained in the same way. The injuries which
> caused the fractures in the leg bones of these patients

were either not observed or were denied when observed.

... There was a striking similarity in the course of events in Case I and Case II of the present study. *In each case unexplained fresh fractures appeared shortly after the patient had arrived home after discharge from the hospital.* In one of these cases the infant was clearly unwanted by both parents and this raised the question of intentional ill-treatment of the infant; the evidence was inadequate to prove or disprove the point. ...

It is possible that some of the fractures in the long bones were caused by the same traumatic forces which were presumably responsible for the subdural hematomas. (pp. 172–3, emphasis added)

Note the cautious wording of Caffey's comments. But we have to remember that Caffey was declaring himself in the face of professional scepticism. It must have taken some courage to carry his discussion even as far as he did: the world of medicine was not prepared for it, as is evidenced by the lack of response.

Five years later another radiologist, Dr Frederic Silverman, presented a paper entitled 'The Roentgen manifestations of unrecognised skeletal trauma in infants' at the annual meeting of the American Roentgen Ray Society in Washington, which was subsequently published (Silverman, 1953).

Silverman went further than Caffey. Describing skeletal trauma as 'probably the most common bone "disease" of infancy,' he went on to say:

It is not often appreciated that many individuals responsible for the care of infants and children (who cannot give their own history) may permit trauma and be unaware of it, may recognize trauma but forget or be reluctant to admit it, or may deliberately injure the child and deny it. (p. 413)

11

This is a significantly more confident statement than Caffey felt able to make.

Silverman described cases very similar to those cited by Caffey, and included one which could be regarded as a classic example of early, potentially unrecognized, child abuse:

> The patient was brought to the Children's Hospital at
> seven months of age with the story that thirty hours
> earlier while the mother was ironing at home, an older
> sibling pushed the baby's bassinet and the hot iron fell
> into the bassinet striking the infant on the left shoulder,
> left upper extremity and left chest. A severe burn
> resulted ... The following day a physician suggested
> hospitalization because of the question of fracture of
> the left upper extremity ... At the proximal end of the
> left humerus there was abundant callus formation and
> irregularity of the underlying bone consistent with a
> comminuted fracture in the healing stage ... The
> fracture was thought to be at least seven to ten days old
> and therefore unrelated to the trauma of thirty hours
> earlier ...
> *The roentgen diagnosis of traumatic lesions was strongly
> resisted by pediatricians and orthopedists interested in
> the child.* The day after admission a complete skeletal
> survey was obtained ... In the lower extremities ...
> multiple and healing fractures with extensive callus
> formation were present in most of the major long
> bones ...
> [According to the parents' report] in January 1950 the
> child had several episodes in which the arms and legs
> became caught in the slats of the crib ... In February
> 1950 the mother fell downstairs with the baby in her
> arms. She attempted to shield the baby but did not
> know whether in her excitement she squeezed the
> baby hard or not ... A nineteen month old sibling was

said to play vigorously with the baby, pulling at the
arms and legs. . . .

. . . one month prior to admission the . . . sibling fed the
baby some cotton. The baby choked and the mother
picked her up by the legs, inverted her and shook and
slapped her violently before the baby coughed up the
cotton. Demonstrating the fashion in which she held the
child . . . the mother gave an excellent demonstration of
a crack-the-whip technique . . .

Two months after admission to hospital, relationships
between the patient's mother and the clinic
deteriorated. Attempts were made to follow up the
child through the Social Service Department but these
were unsuccessful as the child died supposedly of
bronchopneumonia 7 September, 1950. Necropsy was
not permitted. (pp. 416–20, emphasis added)

This kind of history, including the implausible explanations
offered by the parents, could be repeated thousands of times. But
even these dubious accounts would not have surfaced had
Silverman not persisted in his examinations of the child. That he
was unable, in the end, to protect his patient, is a reflection of the
inadequacy of child protection laws at that time. His sense of
professional concern and frustration are apparent in the final
paragraph of the extract.

At the same time, in his discussion, Silverman shows a full
awareness of the impact on parents of inappropriate diagnosis,
e.g. (p. 425): 'The suspicion of a traumatic basis for the lesions can
be . . . devastating in its effects on the family of an infant if the
history is not properly elicited', and (p. 426): 'It is of the greatest
importance not to overwhelm those responsible for the care of the
infant with feelings of guilt.'

These quotations from Silverman's paper nicely demonstrate
the dilemma for medical practitioners: responsibility to protect
the child and responsibility to parents to protect them from the

13

tragedy of diagnostic error. It is possible to imagine that these conflicting responsibilities may often have led to a state of professional inertia.

In 1953 Astley, a British radiologist, published a paper describing six cases of babies with puzzling fractures of the long bones which he ascribed to the peculiar fragility of bones in these infants; this despite the fact that some of the babies also suffered retinal separation, bruising, black eyes and compressed vertebrae, as well as fractures that could not be ascribed to the presumed fragility. Again the 'obvious' inference was not being drawn; a state of professional unreadiness to consider the probable explanation.

A paper by Woolley (a paediatrician) and Evans (a radiologist) in 1955 carried the story a stage further. They were much more definite about the role of parental responsibility in the twelve cases they described, commenting:

> An extremely important point to be noted is that when
> these infants were removed from their environments
> for periods varying from a week to several months no
> new lesions developed and those that were already
> present healed at the expected rate. (p. 541)

In their clinical practice Woolley and Evans had become increasingly convinced of the need to remove children from potentially abusing environments; and increasingly aware of their limited powers to do so:

> Initially we made the parents aware we were not
> satisfied things were entirely peaceful in their
> respective households and, at the same time, indicated
> that we were available in a purely nonpunitive role for
> any help we could provide. Later we attempted to
> enlist the assistance of various agencies including the
> women's division of the police department, in an effort
> to accelerate investigation, but this was largely

abandoned after two families removed themselves rapidly beyond our control and another infant actually died of head injuries while under surveillance. It has become our policy at the moment to attempt by a variety of fortuitous efforts to obtain removal of the child from the household and only then to proceed with investigation of the circumstances surrounding the environment. *It is often difficult for the physician to realize that parents have certain legally well-defined rights that cannot be superseded by his opinion or judgment. This appears to be especially true where the aggrieved party is an infant because, obviously, there is no complainant and rarely a witness.* (p. 542, emphasis added)

This quotation comes almost a decade after Caffey's original paper. With hindsight one might have thought that Woolley and Evans had already made the situation perfectly clear. But as any student of research literature knows, there is a considerable latency between findings being published in academic and professional journals and the implications surfacing in the public consciousness.

The legislative response to the legal vacuum described by the authors was not to be filled for almost another decade. The response, when it came, was rapid and massive. Why the delay?

The answer can be approached by asking another question: what did the evidence amount to? A handful of papers describing a handful of cases and hedged round with qualifications. Today we can read these papers with the knowledge that what they revealed was only a tiny fraction of the problem. We know what should have been inferred. What makes it worse is the knowledge that it is precisely those inarticulate infants referred to by Woolley and Evans who are *most* likely to experience physical abuse. For example, Creighton and Noyes (1989), analysing a UK sample of 4,037 children registered as being physically abused in the period 1983–87, found that 495 (12 per cent) were aged *under* one year and 1,897 (47 per cent) were under five years. The figures represent roughly 10 per cent of total registrations in England and Wales of reported and presumably confirmed cases (see also Table 3.3 in Chapter 3).

In 1956, Dr John Caffey, who had published the original paper, was invited to address the Annual Congress of the British Institute of Radiology in London, his paper subsequently being published (Caffey, 1957). With more support for, and recognition of, his work – of which the invitation to speak to UK radiologists was evidence – Caffey was a great deal more outspoken in his criticism of his medical colleagues, in particular of their search for far-fetched explanations in cases that were 'clinically silent' – a phrase coined by Silverman. Caffey comments:

> In the diagnostic study of infants and children trauma is generally not considered, unless it has been offered voluntarily in the medical history. Paediatricians, faced with unexplained pain and swelling in the extremities, in the absence of a history of injury, customarily set out on an elaborate search for lesions produced by more sophisticated causal agents such as vitamin deficiencies, metabolic imbalances, infections, neoplasms, reticuloendothelical proliferations, prenatal disturbances, and chromosomal injuries contracted in earlier generations. Simple direct mechanical injury often receives short shrift by those bent on solving the mysteries of more exotic diseases.
> (p. 225)

Strong words indeed. And if Caffey is critical of paediatricians he is equally emphatic about the vulnerability of young children: 'too often the infant or child can neither give witness to nor complain about his own injury; and his adult informant may either omit the story of trauma because it is unknown to him, or conceal it intentionally ...' (p. 226) and he concludes (p. 238): 'correct early diagnosis of injury may be the only means by which the abused youngsters can be removed from their traumatic environment and their wrongdoers punished.'

Following this, papers dealing with essentially the same topic appeared every year in the medical literature (Fisher, 1958; Miller, 1959; Altman and Smith, 1960; Gwinn, Lewin and Peterson, 1961). Which brings us back to where this chapter began: the publication year of the paper by Kempe and his associates. If the professional momentum had increased, so, gradually, had public receptivity to the situation portrayed in the rather stilted language of medical research journals.

There is essentially nothing new in Kempe's 1962 paper. It provides a comprehensive review and an extended discussion; but it is vigorous in its denunciation of physicians who have not faced up to the diagnostic challenge. Perhaps we should give the author the last word:

> ... there is a reluctance on the part of many physicians
> to accept the radiologic signs as indications of
> repetitive trauma and possible abuse. This reluctance
> stems from the emotional unwillingness of the
> physician to consider abuse as the cause of the child's
> difficulty and also because of an unfamiliarity with
> certain aspects of fracture healing so that he is unsure
> of the significance of the lesions that are present. To
> the informed physician, the bones tell a story that the
> child is too young or too frightened to tell. (p. 18)

3

THE SCALE OF PHYSICAL ABUSE

The focus of this book is the physical ill-treatment of children. But child-protection services in the 1990s are concerned with much more than direct physical abuse, although in the 1960s and 1970s the primary concern of such services was non-accidental injury, as one might infer from the previous chapter.

In the UK since the mid-1970s, suspected cases of child abuse and neglect have been required to be referred to Social Services Departments. They are investigated and are usually the subject of a case conference which considers the evidence and decides what professional action is necessary: which may include placing the child and family's name on the Child Protection Register.

The percentage breakdown of numbers of children on these Registers in England for the year ending 31 March 1991 is given below in Figure 3.1 (Department of Health, 1992, p. 9).

The category of *sexual abuse* here mainly relates to incidents occurring within the family, although most sexual abuse occurs *outside* the family (Gillham, 1991; Howitt, 1992). The category of *neglect* covers health and safety problems (accidental injury, care, cleanliness and nutrition) which are the result of parental *omission* rather than *commission* (as in the case of *non*-accidental injury). *Emotional abuse* is difficult to define but is probably most readily understood in terms of mental cruelty. The *grave concern* category is relatively new and poses some problems.

Until 1987 in England, Child Protection Registers were known as Child *Abuse* Registers, and the equivalent to *grave concern* were the *at risk* categories. There is, however, wide disagreement and

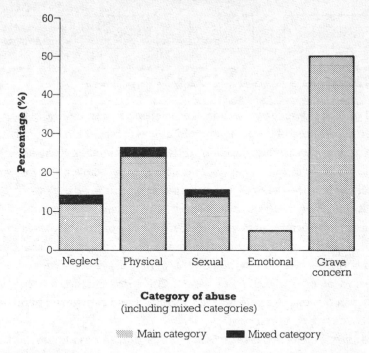

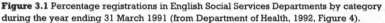

Figure 3.1 Percentage registrations in English Social Services Departments by category during the year ending 31 March 1991 (from Department of Health, 1992, Figure 4).

considerable variation in the usage of the new category. In England the variation is enormous and there is some question as to whether 'grave concern' is being used as an alternative to other categories: see Brown (1992) in Creighton (*op. cit.*).

According to the Department of Health survey previously cited (D of H, 1992), of the 109 Social Services Departments in England, five had more than 70 per cent of their registrations in this category, three had fewer than 10 per cent, and three departments did not use the category at all. This great variation in classification is only part of the difficulty in arriving at an estimate of the true scale of child abuse. Cases have first to come to professional attention. Consider Figure 3.2.

Not all abuse is detected, or recognized for what it is; not all abuse that *is* detected is reported to child-protection agencies; not

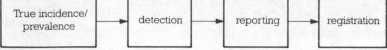

Figure 3.2 The relationship between true incidence and registration.

all of those cases reported are registered. Yet, in the UK at least, our knowledge of the scale of child abuse is based almost entirely on those cases which appear on Child Protection Registers. *It follows that the true scale of child abuse is not known.* All we can talk about is the incidence of *reported* and *registered* cases.

A definition of terms is necessary here. 'Incidence' and 'prevalence' are terms borrowed from medical epidemiology. *Prevalence* refers to the number of cases in the population at any one time; *incidence* refers to the number of *new* cases occurring over a period of time (usually one year). The term 'incidence' as it is used in this chapter refers to the reported and registered number of cases in a one-year period.

There is almost no research on the true prevalence and incidence of child abuse. The exceptions are studies by Murray Straus and his associates in the US, which are reviewed later in this chapter; and there are important limitations to these (Straus, 1979; Straus and Gelles, 1986).

Until 1990, incidence figures for England (and Wales) were extrapolations from data collated by the NSPCC and based on their approximately 10 per cent representation in child-protection services (Creighton, 1985; Creighton and Noyes, 1989; Creighton, 1992). These studies remain a unique source of data on child abuse in England and Wales because of the range of information provided, and the analysis of relationships between the different kinds of data and other information available at a national level (employment levels; social class membership; family composition; and so on). It is to be regretted that this long-standing study of trends in child abuse – over a period of seventeen years – has come to an end at a time when child abuse appears to be increasing.

Following on from a recommendation of the Cleveland Inquiry

Report (DHSS, 1988), the Department of Health now collects data on children registered from all Social Work Departments in England (but not Wales or Scotland) and these are published in the form of Annual Reports (D of H, 1990, 1991b, 1992). These data are valuable but severely restricted because no information is provided about the nature of the abuse, apart from the category of registration, or the parental or social circumstances of the children. The reports are simply a 'statistical' record of the number of children registered, by category, and according to their 'legal' status, for example whether or not they were in care.

The most recent (1992) Department of Health Report provides a starting point (Table 3.1).

This gives some idea of the relative importance of the categories and of that proportion of the child population which reached a level of professional concern sufficient to warrant registration (approximately 0.25 per cent, or one child in 400).

However, this rate varies considerably according to the age and sex of the child (Table 3.2 from D of H, 1992).

Two things are apparent from this table:

1 Children under five (and particularly those under one) are much more likely to be registered than children over five;
2 Boys under five are *slightly* more likely to be registered than girls; after that age the reverse is the case (and more significantly so).

Table 3.1 Rounded numbers, percentages and rates of registration in English Social Services Departments during the year ended 31 March 1990 and 1991 by recorded category (from D of H, 1992, Table 1.5)

Category of abuse	Number	1990 %	Rate	Number	1991 %	Rate
Neglect	3700	14	0.34	3300	12	0.31
Physical abuse	7100	26	0.65	6700	24	0.62
Sexual abuse	4200	15	0.38	3900	14	0.36
Emotional abuse	1200	4	0.11	1300	5	0.12
Grave concern	11800	44	1.08	14100	50	1.30

Note: Percentages exceed 100 because children in 'mixed' categories are counted more than once.

Table 3.2 Numbers and rates of registration in English Social Services Departments during the year ending 31 March 1991, by age and sex (from D of H, 1992, Table 1.1)

	Age on registration					
	Under 1	1–4	5–9	10–15	16 and over	Total
Numbers (1):						
Boys	2100	4300	4000	3000	300	13700
Girls	1900	4000	4000	4100	600	14600
Total	4000	8300	8000	7100	900	28300
Rates (2):						
Boys	6.40	3.34	2.58	1.71	0.41	2.46
Girls	5.95	3.25	2.75	2.46	0.96	2.76
Total	6.18	3.29	2.66	2.08	0.68	2.61

Notes:
1 Figures may not add due to rounding
2 Rates are per 1,000 population in each age and sex group

The age and gender-related difference is due almost entirely to the greater proportion of girls over the age of four who are registered as sexually abused.

As we know from the previous chapter it was revelations about non-accidental injury to very young children – the 'battered child syndrome' – which originally focused attention on the problem of child abuse. In the UK this age-group appears to remain the most vulnerable or at least, the one that is given priority concern. It should be noted, however, that the age-pattern appears to have changed in the US; this is discussed later in the chapter.

The unique value of the NSPCC research reports, already referred to, is that quite apart from the wealth of supplementary detail, which makes interpretation more meaningful, they also provide *longitudinal* data about trends in child abuse in England and Wales. This gives us some idea whether child abuse has decreased following the increase in public awareness, legislative response and the improved provision of child protection services.

Figure 3.3 (from Creighton, 1992) shows the injury rate for 0- to 4-year-olds from 1973–90.

The figure shows an increase in injury rate between 1974 and 1975 followed by a marked decrease in 1976. Following the DHSS

Rate per 1,000

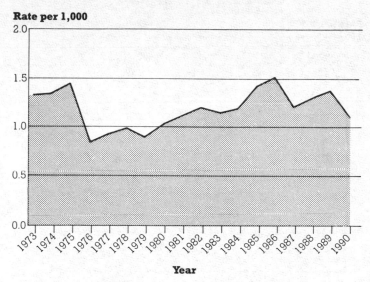

Year

Figure 3.3 Injury rate for 0- to 4-year-olds in England and Wales: registered cases in NSPCC sample (from Creighton, 1992, Figure 8).

(1974) circular, 1975 was the year when registers were established throughout the country. There appears to have been an immediate effect with the establishment of the registers, which was a direct consequence of the tragic death of Maria Colwell (see p. 41), where the Inquiry Report (DHSS, 1973) revealed fundamental inadequacies in professional communication and supervision.

Note that, post-1978, as the world recession began to bite, injury rates showed a general, if erratic, tendency to increase. There is certainly no evidence, at this level, of a continuous improvement in the situation. It may be that the *regulating* effect of register establishment was immediate (because the previous situation was so inadequate) but had little to contribute to further improvements. This effect is more dramatically apparent if we consider the *fatal and serious injury rate* to the same age-group over the same period of time (Figure 3.4).

One would expect that central registers, to which professionals could turn to check whether a child or family was 'known', would

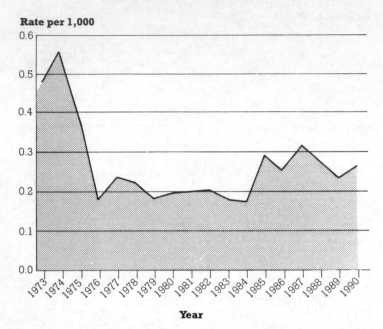

Figure 3.4 Fatal and serious injury for 0- to 4-year-olds in England and Wales: registered cases in NSPCC sample (from Creighton, 1992, Figure 9).

provide some protection at the level of serious injury. Commenting on this function Creighton (1992) says:

> Registers, as part of the whole system of child protection, were instituted to help prevent the deaths or serious impairment of children due to abuse. Before they were set up abusive families were known to 'hospital shop' – take their injured child to different hospitals with each fresh injury, so that suspicion did not build up. Skinner and Castle (1969) propounded a theory of 'an increasing spiral of severity' of these injuries. Registers were designed to act as a central record of information for an area. Each hospital would contact the register when a suspicious injury to a child was presented to them, and be able to see whether there was any previous knowledge of the child or

24

family. In this way it would be possible to intervene at an earlier stage in the spiral. *The rate of seriously and fatally injured children registered is a very good measure of how successfully the child protection system is working in an area* (pp. 65–6, emphasis added)

On this basis, after initial effects, we do not appear to have been very successful. This issue is discussed further in the chapter dealing with child fatalities (Chapter 4) and in the final chapter dealing with issues of prevention.

Over the same period (and this trend may reflect what has happened in the US) the average age of children physically injured who are brought to the attention of the authorities has increased steadily (Figure 3.5).

Over a sixteen-year period the average age of children registered for physical injury has almost doubled – from 3 years 8 months in 1975 to 7 years 1 month in 1990.

Noting that boys are consistently more likely to be physically injured, Creighton links the increasing injury rate for older children to major changes in family composition generally, but particularly in relation to this group. For example, Butler and Golding

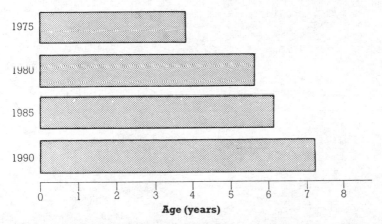

Figure 3.5 Average age of physically injured children in England and Wales: NSPCC sample (from Creighton, 1992, Figure 10).

(1986) in a longitudinal follow-up study of a national cohort of children found that at the age of 5 over 90 per cent of children were living with both natural parents. Creighton (1992) comments: 'If the data are limited to similar social classes to the registered children, the percentage living with both natural parents falls to 73 per cent. Just over a third (36 per cent) of the registered children were living with both their natural parents' (p. 25).

The pie charts in Figure 3.6 show very clearly the shift in the parental situation of injured children over the period 1975–90.

Looking specifically at the aggregated data for 1988–90 the

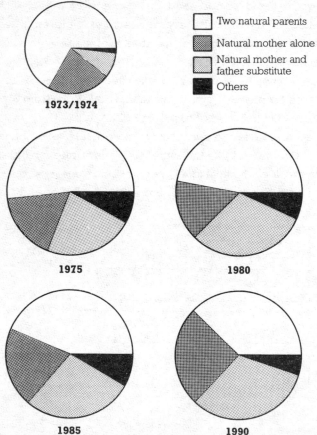

Figure 3.6 The parental situation of injured children in England and Wales 1975–90: NSPCC sample (from Creighton, 1992, Figure 11).

Table 3.3 Parental situation of physically injured children in England and Wales 1988–90 combined: NSPCC sample (from Creighton, 1992, Table 10)

Reason for registration	Parental situation						
	2 NPs No. (%)	NMA No. (%)	NM & Fas No. (%)	NFA No. (%)	NF & MoS No. (%)	Other No. (%)	Total %
Physical injury	972 (35)	649 (23)	735 (26)	84 (3)	92 (3)	69 (3)	(100)

2NPs	–	Two natural parents
NMA	–	Natural mother alone
NM & FaS	–	Natural mother and father substitute
NFA	–	Natural father alone
NF & MoS	–	Natural father and mother substitute
Other	–	Includes relatives, foster parents and other parental situations

parental situation of physically injured children is as shown in Table 3.3.

Is this radical difference from the norm a major factor in the physical abuse of children? The answer is: yes, but not entirely as one might expect. We know that stepfathers and father substitutes are more likely than natural fathers to be involved in the sexual abuse of their partner's children (see Gillham, 1991, p. 22), but it would be wrong to assume that they are more involved in the physical abuse of children. Table 3.4 summarizes the data from

Table 3.4 Suspected perpetrator by type of abuse in England and Wales 1988–90 combined: NSPCC sample (from Creighton, 1992, Table 17)

Perpetrator	Physical Injury		
	No.	(%)	(% l.w.)
Natural mother	831	(30)	(33)
Natural father	813	(29)	(61)
Both	93	(3)	(4)
Stepmother	24	(1)	(40)
Stepfather	220	(8)	(63)
Mother substitute	13		(10)
Father substitute	275	(10)	(59)
Sibling	32	(1)	
Other relative	42	(2)	
Other	111	(4)	
Total	2454	(88)	
No information	332	(12)	

l.w. = living with

the NSPCC study (Creighton, 1992) for the period 1988–90 combined.

From these figures it would appear that father substitutes are no more likely than natural fathers to be involved in physical abuse. However, this finding is in contrast to previous years in the NSPCC study (Creighton, 1992, p. 33) and to data from the US (Russell and Trainor, 1984, p. 26), although the difference is not large. The involvement of father substitutes is, however, greater in cases of severe and fatal physical injury, as is the involvement of men in general (see Chapter 4).

Contrary to popular assumption, natural mothers are as likely as natural fathers to injure their children (slightly more so). This is a consistent finding in the literature but needs to be qualified in two respects.

Firstly, as Table 3.5 shows, women are *eight* times as likely to be single parents as men and this situation is strongly associated with increased rates of child abuse. Secondly, women still bear the brunt of child care in our society: their *exposure* to the stresses and strains of child-rearing is disproportionate.

Who does the abusing, and who gets abused, varies according to the age and sex of the child. Briefly, up to the age of about ten, boys are more likely to be injured than girls (this being true of babies as well). See Table 3.5 from Creighton (1992).

Both natural and substitute fathers are more likely to be involved in the physical abuse of children over ten (Creighton, 1992, p. 33). Rosenthal (1988), in an analysis of 30,901 confirmed reports of abuse and neglect filed with the Colorado Central

Table 3.5 Age and gender of physically injured children in England and Wales 1988–90 combined: NSPCC sample (from Creighton, 1992, Table 9)

	Under 1 year		0–4 years		5–9 years		10–14 years		15+ years	
	No.	(%)	No.	(%)	No.	%	No.	(%)	No.	(%)
Male	182	(57)	686	(57)	416	(62)	331	(50)	74	(31)
Female	138	(43)	516	(43)	256	(38)	336	(50)	162	(68)

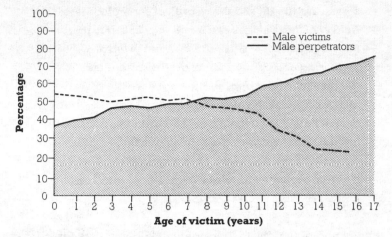

Figure 3.7 Percentage of male victims and male perpetrators of physical abuse filed with the Colorado Central Registry for Child Protection from 1977–84 (from Rosenthal, 1988, Figure 1).

Registry for Child Protection produced the age/gender graph for male victims and male perpetrators of physical abuse shown in Figure 3.7.

Rosenthal comments: 'Male adolescents are abused much less often ... because they can hit back. In particular, females' abuse of male adolescents becomes a rare event; the balance of physical power is with the adolescent' (p. 271).

THE ECONOMIC AND SOCIAL CONDITIONS OF ABUSIVE FAMILIES

The world economic conditions of the past decade or more have provided a kind of 'natural research' setting for elucidating what characterizes abusive families, and probable contributory factors.

Writing in the mid-1980s and commenting on an analysis of some 6,532 cases placed on Child Abuse Registers maintained by the NSPCC in England, Creighton (1985) observed:

> The year 1979 marked the beginning of both the
> cutbacks in resources available to the personal social

29

services in the UK and the growth of unemployment. *Neither of these factors can be directly linked to the increase in physical child abuse shown in this study.* Increasing competition for scarce resources and decreasing work opportunities will have the severest effects on the most vulnerable members of the community. The young, poorly educated parents of large families with few skills to offer in the job market are most at risk in such an economic climate. The children of such parents are over-represented on child abuse registers. (p. 427, emphasis added)

By the end of the decade Creighton (1992) reports that 64 per cent of the male caretakers of registered children in the NSPCC sample were unemployed, at a time when 95 per cent of fathers with dependent children were in paid employment (OPCS, 1991a). In this respect, therefore, abusive families were a quite different population from the nation at large. Of the fathers who *were* employed fewer than one-fifth were in non-manual occupations, compared with more than two-fifths nationally (OPCS, 1992a). This predominance of abusive fathers in manual occupations, particularly unskilled and semi-skilled ones, is a pattern widely reported internationally (Pelton, 1978) and raises the question of reporting bias, which is discussed in Chapter 5.

In summary, the parents of physically abused children are more likely to be: lone or in a 'reconstituted' partnership, unemployed and of low socioeconomic status (with presumably lower levels of education: see Creighton, 1992, pp. 27–8). They are also more likely to be young; and to have a criminal record. Creighton reports that 33 per cent of the mothers in the NSPCC sample were aged less than 20 at the time of the birth of the registered child in the case of physical injury (and percentages were high in all categories of abuse and neglect). The equivalent percentage nationally for those in unskilled occupations was only 5 per cent (OPCS, 1989). In other words, the mothers of physically abused children were almost seven times more likely to have been a teenage mother. The interest of this statistic is that the mothers were not usually teenagers at the time of the maltreatment incident. Miller (1984) commenting on a secondary analysis of data collected in the US National Study of the Incidence and Severity of Child Abuse and Neglect, and looking at parents who were teenagers *at the time of the incident*, found that maltreatment was more common in this category but observed: 'these findings were not surprising considering that children 2 years old and younger, who predominated among children belonging to teenage mothers ... were most often found to suffer fatal or serious injuries ...' (p. 555).

The NSPCC data suggest that even in the medium to long term, teenage motherhood is not a good start to parenting.

A characteristic of abusive parents, particularly fathers and father substitutes, is that they are more likely to have a criminal record. Creighton (*op. cit.*) reports that this was true in the case of 37 per cent of fathers and 12 per cent of mothers of physically injured children, this being considerably higher than the national average (Home Office, 1990).

Being a single parent or unemployed has its own stresses; financial hardship adds to them, and the correlation is high. Consider the following table (3.6) taken from the UK *General Household Survey 1990* (OPCS, 1992a). This shows the average weekly income of single parents with children, compared with normal two-parent families. The difference is dramatically obvious.

Next consider the percentage of mothers of young children in employment, according to whether or not they are single parents (Table 3.7).

It is worth noting that Brown and Harris (1978) found that being employed was one of the factors that appeared to protect women from the onset of depression in the face of stressful life events. But it is possible to be too 'psychological' in the explanation of the behaviour of people who suffer severe financial hardship;

Table 3.6 Usual gross weekly income for families with dependent children in the UK 1990 (from OPCS, 1992a, Table 2.40)

Families with dependent children*

Family type		£0.01–£100.00	£100.01–£150.00	£150.01–£200.00	£200.01–£250.00	£250.01–£300.00	£300.01–£350.00	£350.01 or over	Base = 100%†
				Usual gross weekly household income					
Married couple	%	4	6	6	9	10	11	55	1729
Lone mother	%	54	16	10	6	4	3	7	452
Single	%	70	12	6	3	3	1	5	155
Widowed	%	[38]	[29]	[4]	[12]	[12]	[4]	[0]	24
Divorced	%	41	18	15	9	5	3	8	170
Separated	%	53	17	9	5	3	6	8	103
Lone father	%	[21]	[12]	[6]	[12]	[6]	[12]	[32]	34
All lone parents	%	51	16	10	7	4	4	8	486

* Dependent children are persons aged under 16, or aged 16–18 in full-time education, in the family unit and living in the household.
† Bases exclude cases where income is not known.

Table 3.7 Economic status of women with dependent children in the UK 1990 (from OPCS, 1992a, Table 2.38)

Women with dependent children*

Family Type		Working full time	Working part time	Total working†	Unemployed	Inactive	Base = 100%
Married mother	%	21	42	63	3	34	2427
Lone mother	%	19	22	42	6	53	542
Single	%	12	14	26	8	65	185
Widowed	%	[25]	[19]	[44]	[6]	[50]	32
Divorced	%	23	30	56	4	40	205
Separated	%	20	21	41	5	54	120

* Dependent children are persons aged under 16, or aged 16–18 in full-time education, in the family unit and living in the household.
† Total includes those on Government Schemes and those whose hours of work were not known.

particularly when one has not experienced it oneself. As we shall see in Chapter 6, poverty is not a sufficient explanation of child abuse but the association is a strong one; and politically uncomfortable.

Following on from the Second National Family Violence Survey in the US (Straus and Gelles, 1986), Gelles (1989) explored the question of whether it was being *single-handed* or being *poor* that explained the internationally found association between single-parenthood and child physical abuse. He comments:

> Absent from the reports of high rates of child abuse in single-parent homes is any detailed discussion of the reasons for the higher rates. One hypothesis is that the risk of abuse is greater because the single head of household is alone. It is assumed that lack of a partner because of divorce, separation, abandonment, death, or out-of-wedlock birth entails difficulties in meeting the time-consuming and stressful demands of child rearing and that this increases the risk of violence and abuse. We shall refer to this explanation as the 'parent-absent hypothesis'.
>
> Single parents not only have to meet the demands of child rearing on their own; they tend to meet these demands with far fewer economic resources than are available in dual caretaker homes. Nearly 90% of single-parent households are headed by women (Bureau of the Census, 1985) and approximately half of all mother-only families are poor (Garfinkel and McLanahan, 1986). Since low income has been found to be related to high rates of violence and abuse of children (Straus, Gelles and Steinmetz, 1980), it is possible that poverty, and not the stress of raising children alone, puts single-parent households at high risk of abuse. We refer to this explanation as the 'economic deprivation hypothesis'. (p. 493)

What Gelles found was that among single *mothers* a high rate of poverty explained their high rate of violence, but that there was an exceptionally high rate of violence among single *fathers* at *all* income levels, but especially among the poorest. He concludes:

> The documented high risk of abuse and maltreatment in single-parent households demands the development of treatment and policy programs that can support single parents and protect their children. Such programs must be aimed at ameliorating the devastating consequences of poverty among single parents, mothers and fathers alike. (p. 500)

The extreme character of the relationship between poverty and being a single parent, *particularly a lone mother*, is readily apparent from the UK data reported in Table 3.7. For lone mothers the ratio of income is in almost exact inverse relationship to that for married couples living together. The poverty association for lone fathers is not so extreme.

NATIONAL RESEARCH IN THE US

Most research and, it has to be said, the best research on child abuse has been carried out in the US. Research also began earlier, particularly at the level of the collation of national level statistics. It is on these large-scale surveys that we shall concentrate here.

The first such survey in the US was that of Gil (1970). He collated every case of physical abuse reported through legal channels in 1967 and 1968 – over 20,000 cases. This was the first substantial epidemiological study and it changed the perspective on child abuse, which had hitherto been dominated by clinical studies. Notably, Gil's analysis highlighted the role of social disadvantage and poverty in the etiology of child abuse.

In 1974 governmental responsibility was given to the newly created National Center on Child Abuse and Neglect to set up a national study on child neglect and abuse reporting. This was carried out for NCCAN by the American Humane Association with the following aims:

- to determine the number of families, alleged perpetrators and involved children of official reports of child maltreatment;
- to determine the source of referral and the geographic distribution of official reports;
- to describe the characteristic of families, perpetrators and children involved in official reports and, where possible, compare them against the general population;
- to describe the response of the child protective services system;
- to identify and describe trends in the reporting data.

(Russell and Trainor, 1984, p. 8)

Most states co-operated in this venture and the first returns (for 1976) were made in 1977. Because of variations in categories and individual data elements between different states, a *minimal data set* of common elements and categories was developed in 1978. More than fifteen years later nothing comparable (other than the now defunct NSPCC study on a much smaller scale) has been developed in the UK.

By 1982 no less than 458,000 *annual* case reports were included in the data base and these, together with the data for the years since 1976 were the subject of a national study of trends in child abuse and neglect (Russell and Trainor, 1984). In addition the American Humane Association produces an annual statistical summary report.

In general, US findings are broadly in line with UK data. But there are important differences.

The ratio of female to male perpetrators of abuse *and* neglect is higher (60.8 per cent female to 39.2 per cent male: Russell and Trainor, 1984, p. 25). But this appears to be linked to the much higher proportion of single-parent families in the US – 25 per cent according to the *General Household Survey 1989* (OPCS, 1991a); and to the fact that neglect is mainly characteristic of female-headed families: see Table 3.8 from Russell and Trainor (1984).

Table 3.8 also shows the same strong association with unemployment as in the UK.

An apparent major difference between US and UK statistics is in the proportion of physically abused children at each age-level. In the UK this is predominantly a category involving *very* young children (see Table 3.2 earlier in this chapter). Describing the situation in the US Russell and Trainor (*op. cit.*, p. 23) comment: 'Perhaps surprising to most people is the fact that physical injury affects a sizeable proportion of all age-groups, but that the highest rate of physical injury is found among the oldest children.' Table 3.9 shows this age association, as a percentage of all reports.

We know that young children who are subject to violence are more likely to sustain serious injuries (this being especially true of babies) and the difference may be due to different reporting

Table 3.8 Characteristics of abusive families and neglected families compared to all US families (from Russell and Trainor, 1984, p. 97, Table A–IV–7)

	1981 reported families		
	Neglect only	Abuse only	US population
CHILD CHARACTERISTICS			
Average age (years)	6.82	8.22	9.42
Race			
% white	69.3	74.4	78.6
% black	25.4	19.5	14.7
% other	6.3	6.1	6.7
CARETAKER CHARACTERISTICS			
Median age (years)	28.93	31.03	36.50
FAMILY CHARACTERISTICS			
% female-headed families	52.2	30.8	16.8
% receiving public assistance	47.6	33.7	17.3
% all caretakers unemployed	44.1	23.7	6.5
Average number of children in home	2.23	2.09	1.89
Stress factors			
% economic/physical living conditions	63.8	39.9	N/A
% inadequate housing	18.8	7.0	N/A
% insufficient income	7.3	5.5	N/A

Table 3.9 Child age by type of maltreatment: all reports (1979 and 1982 only) (from Russell and Trainor, 1984, p. 95, Table A–IV–3)

PERCENT OF CHILDREN HAVING EACH MALTREATMENT TYPE*

Child age and year	Physical injury	Sexual maltreatment	Deprivation of necessities	Emotional maltreatment
Birth to 2 years				
1979 (N = 37,577)	15.3%	0.1%	56.3%	4.3%
1982 (N = 75,844)	17.0%	1.4%	61.2%	4.1%
3 to 5 years				
1979 (N = 35,132)	17.4%	3.0%	53.5%	5.3%
1982 (N = 65,576)	18.3%	4.8%	56.5%	5.4%
6 to 11 years				
1979 (N = 64,044)	15.7%	4.7%	54.1%	6.1%
1982 (N = 107,162)	17.9%	6.0%	55.1%	6.2%
12 to 17 years				
1979 (N = 49,481)	20.3%	9.1%	41.0%	8.7%
1982 (N = 78,681)	21.8%	10.5%	42.3%	8.1%

* Does not add up to 100.0 per cent across rows because each child could have experienced more than one type of maltreatment, because 'other' maltreatments have been excluded, and because 'multiple' maltreatments have been excluded.

criteria for 'minor or unspecified physical injury' which make up the great majority of reports. Since the US study does not report on age differences in major physical injury, we can only speculate. It may be that, particularly in the US, there has been a shift in attitude to the physical punishment of children so that the criterion for 'abuse' has shifted. Two prominent researchers into family violence in the US certainly believe that this is so. Straus and Gelles (1986) comment:

> ... new standards are evolving in respect to how much violence parents can use in child-rearing ...
>
> Changed standards are also the real force behind the child abuse reporting laws. Were it not for these changing standards, the reporting laws would not have been enacted; or, if enacted, they would tend to be ignored. (p. 466–7)

REPORTED INCIDENCE AND TRUE INCIDENCE

A repeated theme of official reported incidence studies is that: 'the relation between official reports and all incidents of child maltreatment is unknown' (Russell and Trainor, 1984, p. 11).

The only empirical studies that have attempted to assess the true scale of child physical abuse, employing a nationally representative sample, are those of Murray Straus and his colleagues at the University of New Hampshire's Family Violence Research Program, from which much of the most important research on child abuse has emanated (Straus, 1979; Straus, Gelles and Steinmetz, 1980; Straus and Gelles, 1986; Gelles, 1989).

In their first, 1979 study they interviewed, equally, fathers and mothers in 1,146 families with a child aged from 3 to 17 at home. This was an investigation of violence in the family, not just violence towards children. Parents were asked whether, during the preceding twelve months they had used violence towards the child more severe than pushing, shoving, slapping and throwing things, i.e. had they ever 'kicked, bit, punched, hit with an object, beaten up the child, or used a knife or a gun (in the sense of having actually tried to stab or shoot the child)' (Straus, 1989, p. 215). One can only wonder at the temerity of American research-ers!

Straus and his colleagues found that even when they excluded the category 'hit with an object' they still found an estimated national incidence of two million children a year who were physically abused as against official reports of 250,000. What accounts for the difference? Straus suggests two main reasons:

> (1) The NCCAN figures are based on incidents which
> come to official attention. This leaves out the vast
> number of cases in which physical abuse is suspected
> but not reported, as well as the equally vast number of
> cases in which a child is injured but there is no
> suspicion of abuse.
> (2) Probably the most important reason why our rates
> are so much higher is that our data is based on violent
> acts carried out, rather than on injuries produced.
> Fortunately children are resilient. Many is the child
> who has been thrown against a wall and who simply
> bounces off with at most a bruise. Only the relatively
> rare instances in which a concussion occurs stand even
> a chance of being suspected of parental abuse. (Straus,
> 1979, p. 215)

Straus points out that his estimate is likely to be conservative because:

- data on violence to children under three (a high-risk category) were not obtained;
- these were self-reports by parents to a stranger doing a survey;

- only *one* parent was interviewed about *one* child in the family;
- single-parent families (a high-risk group) were not included;
- some forms of physical abuse, e.g. burning, were not included.

A follow-up survey by Straus and Gelles (1986) found an essentially similar pattern but lower overall rates.

Although these studies apply to the US and we must be cautious about generalizing the scale of the findings to the UK, they do emphasize the very important point that those incidents of child physical abuse that come to official attention because of the degree of *injury* must be a gross underestimate of the amount of *violence* towards children and within families. Child abuse is a routine occurrence; in a sense it can be seen as 'normal'. Otherwise how could it be so pervasive? We know that the cases officially recognized are but a fraction of all abusive incidents. It is only the most extreme cases that attract the notice of the public at large.

4
FATAL CHILD ABUSE

Maria was not seen alive outside the circle of her own family after ... 27 December and we have only Mrs Kepple's unchallenged account of those last days, but we feel some aspects of it should be recorded. In brief she told us that on 2 January 1973 she returned to find Maria with a black eye and Mr Kepple told her that she had fallen downstairs. Two days later she alleged that Mr Kepple started hitting Maria on her legs because she had not used paper in the lavatory and she had tried to stop him and he had been very angry with her also. She had, she told us, made up her mind to tell Miss Lees, having already told Mr Kepple that she would tell her that he and Maria didn't get on. However, on 6 January, which was a Saturday, Mr Kepple came in at 11.30 p.m. and the events which formed the basis of the indictment against Mr Kepple then occurred.

The following morning the Kepples took Maria in the pram to the hospital where she was found to be dead. The post-mortem carried out by Professor Cameron on 11 January showed that she was severely bruised all over the body and head and had sustained severe internal injuries to the stomach. There was a healing fracture of one rib. The bruising, which was described by Professor Cameron as the worst he had ever seen, was of variable age up to 10 to 14 days at most, which was the longest period that bruising might be expected to last, but the

*majority dated from within 48 hours. The majority of the
injuries he described as the result of extreme violence.
The stomach was empty and the body weighed 36 lbs.,
whereas the medical evidence in the case generally
showed that she should for her age and height have
weighed anything between 46 and 50 lbs. or
thereabouts. She had in fact grown one inch and lost
over 5 lbs. since her last medical examination on 4
August 1971, 17 months before her death.*

(Excerpt from: *The Report of the Committee of Inquiry into the Care
and Supervision Provided in Relation to Maria Colwell* (DHSS, 1973),
paras 146 and 147, pp. 59–60)

Nothing focuses public attention and concern like the violent,
abusive, or grossly neglectful death of a child. The public outrage
often leads to rapid political and professional action and, as was
demonstrated in Chapter 1, this is characteristic of the history of
child protection.

The murder of Maria Colwell, described above in the stark
terms of an official report, led to the rapid establishment in the UK
of what were then known as Child Abuse Registers. The death of
even one child under such circumstances is an unarguable reality,
inexcusable by any explanation, the ultimate failure of the child-
protection system. But is the prevention of child-abuse fatalities
really possible? Fatal child abuse continues and it is by no means
certain that it is decreasing.

Inquiry reports, similar to that concerning Maria Colwell, recur
periodically. In the UK the Department of Health (1991a) published *A Study of Inquiry Reports 1980–1989*. It covers nineteen
such investigations. A parallel earlier summary (DHSS, 1982) dealt
with eighteen investigations over the period 1973–81. These were
all 'headline' cases where there was concern about the working of
the child protection services. They represent, of course, but a
small fraction of child homicides.

The more recent of these summaries reflects a greater awareness of the complicated nature of fatal child abuse and less confidence about action. The introduction to the 1991 summary comments:

> What was remarkable in the first decade of inquiries was the coherence of the findings. In the 1980s a more complicated picture emerges. The messages from the last decade of reports may seem depressing but it is understandable where difficult decisions concerning human relationships are being made by professional staff from a number of agencies that tragedies will from time to time occur. (p. iii)

There is a note of acceptance here, stemming from a greater awareness of the near-impossibility of the task. This dilemma is well-summarized in that section of the report concerned with the prediction of abuse, quoting from the report on the death of Liam Johnson:

> It was said to us before we started hearing evidence that if we could suggest ways in which families like this, who in no way stand out from hundreds of others with whom the agencies deal, could somehow be identified before the tragedy occurs it would be an enormous help. It will be clear from the pages that follow that although we suggest ways in which practice might be improved, we have been unable to suggest any infallible method of spotting potential child killers. (p. 63)

Alfaro (1991) in a review of nine US studies of child abuse fatalities puts the issue more bluntly:

> The demand that fatalities and serious harm be prevented assumes that the means of prediction and prevention exist. Hindsight reviews of fatality cases frequently create the impression that the precursors to

death were clearly visible and that a timely and
effective intervention might have saved a life. (p. 219)

CHILD MORTALITY STATISTICS

Child-abuse fatalities are a subset of *all* child deaths and it is here
that we start.

It is conventional to distinguish between *childhood mortality* and
infant mortality. Childhood mortality relates to children aged one
year and over, infant mortality to children aged under one year.
Infant mortality is further subdivided into *stillbirths* (children born
dead), *neonatal deaths* (children born alive but dying within 28
days) and *postneonatal deaths* (children dying after the age of 28
days but before the age of one year).

The reason for these subdivisions by age can be understood by
looking at Figures 4.1 and 4.2, taken from the OPCS publication
Mortality Statistics: Childhood 1988 (OPCS, 1991b). These graphs
repay careful study. Note the following points:

- *infant* mortality rates are greater than *childhood* mortality rates
  by a factor of 10 to 15;
- *male* mortality is consistently greater than *female* mortality;
- there have been general declines in the mortality rates since
  1971, although these show signs of flattening out since the early
  1980s;
- the largest declines have been amongst children aged from 1 to
  4 years and amongst stillbirths and neonatal deaths;
- the decline is very much less in the *post*neonatal period and this
  is especially true in the case of boys;
- by the mid-1980s the postneonatal mortality rate for boys was
  greater than the *neo*natal rate for girls.

These last two observations are mainly accounted for by the
large number of *sudden infant deaths*: almost half of the total
number of postneonatal deaths in England and Wales in 1988 (866
of 1,682 male PNND; 524 of 1,167 female PNND (OPCS, 1991b)).

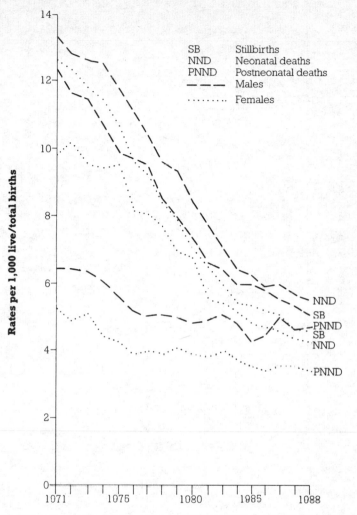

Figure 4.1 Infant mortality, by sex and age 1971–88, England and Wales (from OPCS, 1991b, Figure A).

The percentage assigned to this category has declined since then (OPCS, 1992b, p. xiv) and the possible reasons for this will be considered as part of a discussion of the *Sudden Infant Death Syndrome* (SIDS) later in this chapter.

As noted previously, infancy is the dangerous time of life: life

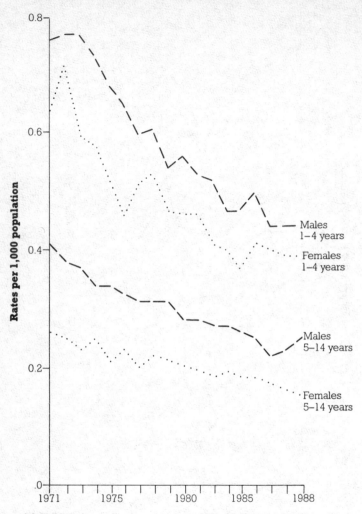

Figure 4.2 Childhood mortality, by sex and age 1971–88, England and Wales (from OPCS, 1991b, Figure B).

expectancy improves dramatically once a child passes the one-year mark, particularly if it is female. The trends described above are general in Western societies. Infant mortality rates for the US for a comparable period are given in Figure 4.3 (from Wilson, 1990, Figure 1).

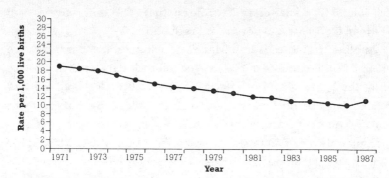

Figure 4.3 Infant mortality rates, United States 1971–87 (derived from Wilson, 1990, Figure 1).

It will be seen that rates and the pattern of gradual decline and levelling out are very similar to the UK statistics.

Infant death rates have changed over time but differentially in relation to socioeconomic class. Figure 4.4 shows infant death rates in social classes I, II, IV and V for babies born within marriage in Scotland from 1971–91 (Registrar General Scotland, 1992). The death rate for infants in social class V (unskilled manual) only twenty years ago was two to three times greater than

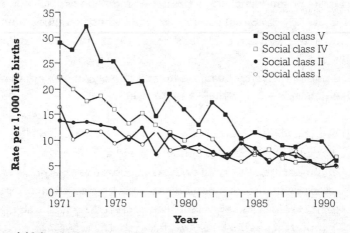

Figure 4.4 Infant death rates in social classes I, II, IV, and V, Scotland 1971–91 (from Registrar General Scotland, 1992, p. 92).

for infants in social class I (professional). The difference is still there in the 1990s, but very much reduced.

Another variable of importance is whether the parents were married at the time of the birth. The Scottish data cited above are only for births *within* marriage. In the returns for England and Wales data are available on social class (by occupation) for births outside marriage where the birth is registered by *both* parents – presumably an advantaged subset of all illegitimate births. Table 4.1 shows infant deaths by father's social class and mother's marital status.

Rates for illegitimate births are enhanced, most significantly for 'manual' social classes where most illegitimate births occur. This differential pattern is one we need to keep in mind.

The dramatic reduction in child mortality and, in particular, *infant* mortality is testimony to advances in medicine and social care. However, the rate of reduction has flattened out during the past decade and it may be that we are coming down to a nucleus of child fatalities that are less easy, perhaps impossible, to prevent. The category we are concerned with here is infant or child homicide, or fatal child abuse.

As noted above, the age-range where mortality has declined *least* is the postneonatal stage (from one month to twelve months). This is the age-range where known child-abuse fatalities tend to cluster; and where some forms of homicide are peculiarly difficult to detect.

In a paper analysing infant death in South Dakota, as compared with the US as a whole, Wilson (1990) comments:

> Among the preventable causes of postneonatal death is homicide that includes child battering and other maltreatment. While all deaths of children are tragic, these deaths seem most sad and must be viewed in part to reflect society's failure to protect the young and support those who face the challenges of caring for children. National estimates indicate that between

48

Table 4.1 Infant deaths by father's social class as defined by occupation and mother's marital status England and Wales 1988–90 (from OPCS, 1992b, p. xvi, Table B)

Social class	All Ages						Mothers aged 25–29					
	Within marriage		Outside marriage registered by both parents		Total within marriage and jointly registered outside marriage		Within marriage		Outside marriage registered by both parents		Total within marriage and jointly registered outside marriage	
	Number	Rate*	Number	Rate*	Number	Rate*	Number	Rate*	Number	Rate*	Number	Rate*
All	11,122	7.3	4,074	10.2	15,196	7.9	3,926	6.4	886	9.3	4,812	6.8
I	794	6.2	66	6.6	860	6.2	256	5.5	18	6.4	274	5.6
II	2,319	6.0	416	7.7	2,735	6.2	807	5.3	105	6.6	912	5.4
IIIN	1,064	6.7	228	9.0	1,292	7.1	421	6.2	60	9.2	481	6.5
IIIM	3,613	7.0	1,561	9.2	5,174	7.6	1,351	6.3	349	8.4	1,700	6.6
IV	1,807	9.1	800	10.4	2,607	9.5	591	7.6	178	10.8	760	8.2
V	766	11.0	602	12.7	1,368	11.7	206	8.5	109	12.3	315	9.5
Other	817	11.9	401	24.3	1,218	14.3	293	10.8	68	20.6	361	11.9

* Rates per 1,000 live births

49

1986 and 1988 over 1,100 children were reported
yearly as fatal victims of child abuse and neglect. To
put this figure in perspective, it can be viewed as
almost equivalent to the number of newborns who die
of congenital heart anomalies. (p. 8)

Using data from the US National Center for Health Statistics
Wilson constructed the following table (Table 4.2) according to
whether postneonatal death could be classified as 'preventable',
'potentially preventable', 'non-preventable', 'unknown' or 'resid-
ual'.

Note that only a quarter of the deaths are classified as 'non-
preventable' and that more than half – including the contentious
classification SIDS – cannot be fully explained.

Zumwalt and Hirsch (1980) introduced the term 'subtle fatal
child abuse' to describe those cases where the homicidal nature
of child fatalities is obscured. They describe six such cases and
comment:

Our recognition of life endangering child abuse cannot
be restricted by conceptions of the classic battered
child syndrome or other well-defined and medically
documented means of lethal maltreatment such as

Table 4.2 Distribution of causes of postneonatal mortality United States
1983–87 (adapted from Wilson, 1990, p. 9, Table 1)

Potentially preventable	
Infections	11.3%
Injury	7.4%
Non preventable	
Congential anomalies	15.9%
Systemic – non-perinatal	9.7%
Unknown	
Sudden Infant Death	35.4%
Systemic – perinatal	7.7%
Ill-defined symptoms	4.0%
Residual	8.8%

Data from the National Center for Health Statistics.
Cause of death data were taken from the International Classification of
Diseases, ninth edition.

starvation or whiplash shaking ... Pathologists must be
mindful that the vulnerability and delicacy of infants
and young children render them susceptible to death
as a direct result of many subtle forms of assault or
from negligence. (p. 167)

As a footnote to this, Mitchel (1989) in a report on fatalities from
the US National Committee for Prevention of Child Abuse points
out that:

Research has consistently found that some percentage
of accidental deaths, child homicides and Sudden
Infant Death Syndrome cases might be more
appropriately labeled as child maltreatment death if
comprehensive investigations were routinely
conducted. (p. 3)

THE SCALE OF FATAL CHILD ABUSE

Bearing in mind the impact on the public conscience of cases of
child abuse resulting in death, one might expect that statistics
were readily available. They are not. In the UK it is not the usual
practice for child-abuse fatalities to be recorded on what are now
called Child *Protection* Registers, so that there is no information on
this important matter in the reports of numbers of children on such
registers published annually by the Department of Health; this
despite the wide recognition that 'the extreme consequence of
child abuse is a dead child' (Pritchard, 1992, p. 663). And, it
should be added, the extreme failure of child protection.

Pritchard, in the paper cited, tries to argue that reductions in
reported infant homicides in England, Wales and Scotland over
the period 1973/74 to 1987/88, as shown in WHO statistics, reflect
the effectiveness of child-protection services. But legal homicide
is filtered by a number of processes, both formal and informal:
cultural norms; administrative, medical, legal and judicial practice. If the WHO statistics are to be believed, for example, there

were *no* infant homicides in Sweden in 1973/74 nor in Ireland in 1987/88. Such statistics are at some distance from the reality.

Childhood mortality statistics for England and Wales are published by the Office of Population Censuses and Surveys, and for Scotland by the General Register Office. These reports classify the causes of death in accordance with the International Statistical Classification of Diseases, Injuries and Causes of Death (ICD)

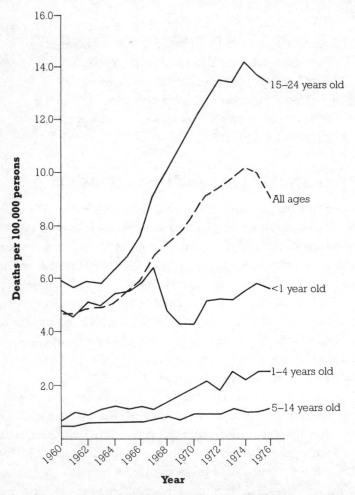

Figure 4.5 Homicide rates for selected age-groups by year and all ages by year, United States 1960–76 (from Jason, Carpenter and Tyler, 1983, p. 196, Figure 1).

(Ninth Revision), which has operated by international agreement from January 1979. Each 'cause' has its own ICD number and these have to be used on official death certificates. In the 1988 report for England and Wales (OPCS, 1991b), against ICD No. E967 (Child battering and other maltreatment) a total of only 16 deaths (included in a total of 21 homicides) are recorded *at this level*. However, it is possible that other child-abuse fatalities are concealed in other, more 'open' categories.

The effect of 'category choice' on official rates is clearly shown in a study by Jason, Carpenter and Tyler (1983) entitled 'Under-recording of infant homicide in the United States'.

Briefly, there was a sudden apparent drop in homicide rates for infants between 1967 and 1969: see Figure 4.5.

Note that homicide rates for infants were the only category to show a decline. The authors suggest that 'the abrupt nature of this decline was artifactual due to changes in related ICD codes and death certificates: in particular the introduction of the category "injuries undetermined whether accidental or purposely inflicted"'. When the 'undetermined' rate is added to the 'homicide' rate, the trend is comparable to trends at other age-levels: see Figure 4.6.

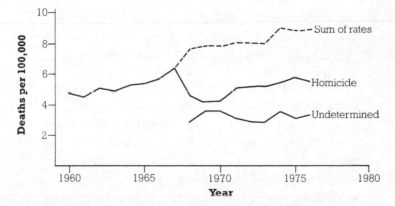

Figure 4.6 Death rates from homicide and deaths undetermined whether homicide or accident for infants less than one year old (from Jason, Carpenter and Tyler, 1983, p. 196, Figure 2).

The summary point is this: we know how many children die. What we are not reliably clear about, *especially* at the level of official statistics is *why*. Which is to say that the true scale of child-abuse fatalities is unknown.

The problem is compounded in the UK by the fact that there is no national agency collecting data from all sources and that local sources (Child Protection Registers) do not routinely record child fatalities. The nearest approximation to such a national agency has been the NSPCC which maintained approximately 10 per cent of registers in England and Wales up to 1990. Creighton (1992) in the final report from this study says (pp. 46–7):

> The NSPCC has always had a policy of registering dead children ... The transition from Child Abuse to Child Protection Registers is likely to lead to the exclusion of dead children from the registration process. They are, after all, no longer in need of protection.

Noting a decline in the number of registered deaths, Creighton makes it clear that this may be a change in practice. The period 1988–90 covers the time when Child Abuse Registers became Child *Protection* Registers.

In the earlier NSPCC study (Creighton and Noyes, 1989) covering the period 1983–87, the deaths of 36 children were notified to the NSPCC registers. The authors comment:

> Twenty-seven of these were registered either after their deaths, or after the injuries which caused their deaths had been inflicted. The remaining nine children were already registered when they died. Seven of these deaths were either natural or accidental: four cot deaths, two children from one family in a house fire and one 13-year-old from scalds incurred accidentally. The cot deaths had initially been registered respectively as 'at risk', neglect, neglect and bruising

and facial bruising. The two children who died in the fire had been registered for neglect and bruising and neglect, and the scalded child from bruising to the body. . . . All twenty-seven fatalities [notified after their deaths] were aged less than five and fifteen of them were less than one-year-old. The average age of the fatalities was 1 year 4.5 months ranging from 0 months to 4 years 2 months. (p. 33)

These data raise the question of the value of registration. Most of the children killed were from families unknown to child protection agencies; and we shall see below that this is typical in the US. And being registered did not serve to protect the other children who died.

We have to conclude that it is not possible to say whether rates for child-abuse fatalities are increasing or decreasing in the UK since reliable data are not available.

Central data collection is managed better in the US and the picture there is of a steady increase in child-abuse fatalities. Mitchel (1989) reports that there was a 36 per cent rise between 1985 and 1988. He points out that very young children were the largest group of victims and adds: 'Of the child-abuse fatalities reported by the states, a majority were two years of age or younger, with an average age of 2.8 years' (p. 3).

A review of nine US studies by Alfaro (1991) found that between 62 per cent and 80 per cent of children who died were two years old or younger.

CHARACTERISTICS OF CHILD ABUSE FATALITIES

The summary table (4.3) from Alfaro (1991) is useful because it pulls together rather unwieldy information which is widely reported elsewhere. We shall expand on this by looking at three other in-depth studies of child-abuse fatalities in the US (Anderson *et al.* (1983); Jason and Andereck (1983); Margolin (1990)).

Table 4.3 Trends in child abuse fatality case characteristics across nine US studies (from Alfaro, 1991, p. 259, Table 3)

Characteristic	Description of trend across studies
Age of child	All studies report young age of child, usually under two or three years old
Sex of child	7 of 9 studies report a majority are boys (53%–67%). Two studies with comparative data found no significant gender differences between fatal and non-fatal cases.
Health of child	Range of health problems reported (27%–67% of cases). Range of handicapped children also ranged widely (2%–29%). The one study with comparative data found no difference between fatal and non-fatal protective cases.
Ethnicity	7 of 9 studies found Black children in high proportion (52%–73%) or in disproportion when compared to general population or entire protective service caseload.
Household composition/ perpetrators	7 of 9 studies found men (fathers, step-fathers, paramours) are involved in a majority of fatality cases (59%–100%).
Age of parents/ perpetrators	Most are in their twenties. Two studies reported that mothers are somewhat younger in fatality cases, but another found this difference is not statistically significant.
Social-economic status of family	The available data indicate a high proportion of poor families, but the two studies with comparative data found this is also true of non-fatal cases.
Parental impairments	Various ranges reported for mental illness (8%–36%), drug addiction (24%–40%), Alcoholism (20%), or substance abuse (14%–27%). But available comparative data shows similiar extent of these problems in non-fatal cases, except for drug use by a father or father substitute.
Family violence	Very limited data, with ranges from 12% to 44% of fatality cases. Two studies with comparative data, however, found similar rates of both fatal and non-fatal cases.
Criminal history	Varying arrest rates reported (29%–60%), but these rates are higher for men than for the mothers involved in fatality cases. The one study with comparative data found significant differences in arrest history of men but not mothers in fatality cases.
Prior abuse or neglect reports	About one-third of the fatality cases, on average, were previously reported, ranging from 20% to 49%. (This range may reflect differences in the extent to which unfounded reports are expunged and the age of state central registers). The three studies with comparative data found the rate of prior reports in fatal and non-fatal cases is similar or not statistically significant.

The study by Jason and Andereck looked at child-abuse fatalities and child homicides in Georgia in the period July 1975 to December 1979. Neglect fatalities were not recorded at that time.

It can be clearly seen from Figure 4.7 that it is children under five and over fifteen who are mainly at risk of fatal assault: primarily from within the family in the case of young children, and from outside the family in the case of adolescents.

The study by Anderson *et al.* was of 267 child deaths associated with abuse *and* neglect in Texas during the period 1975–77. They make the interesting observation (as in the NSPCC study in the UK) that over three-quarters of the families had never come to the attention of the state's child-protection agencies. They also found that *neglect* was as likely to be the cause of death as abuse. They report that abuse was involved in 39 per cent of the child deaths, neglect in 40 per cent, and neglect and abuse combined in 20 per cent of the cases. The median age of these children was 1.8 years compared with 10.1 years for non-fatal child abuse and neglect cases.

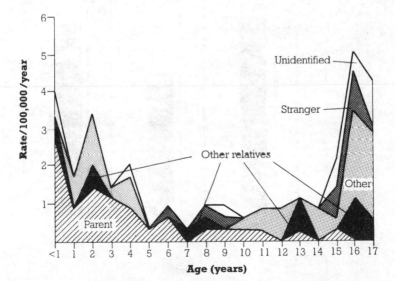

Figure 4.7 Incidence of child homicide by age of victim and by relationship to perpetrator, Georgia, US 1976–79 (from Jason and Andereck, 1983, p. 4, Figure 2).

The focus of this study on *neglect* fatalities is of particular value and the authors comment that their data 'indicate ... that the importance of child neglect associated with child fatalities should not be minimized. Rather child neglect merits greater, not less, attention from a policy and program standpoint' (p. 86). They point to the particular vulnerability of boys in this respect: 'male deaths were more likely to be implicated in cases of neglect or abuse and neglect combined, whereas female deaths were more likely to be implicated in instances of abuse alone' (p. 81). This pattern is shown very clearly in Figure 4.8 from their study.

Margolin analysed 82 child fatalities attributed either to neglect or physical abuse and investigated by the Iowa Department of Human Services. He comments:

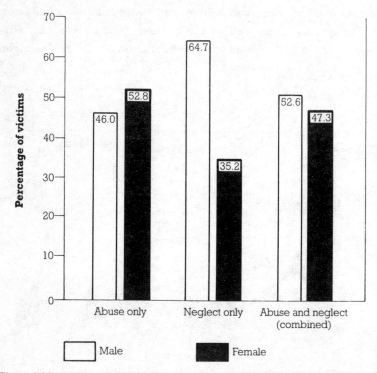

Figure 4.8 Distribution of child fatalities by gender and case finding, Texas 1975–77 (from Anderson *et al.*, 1983, p. 82, Figure 1).

A stereotype associated with child neglect represents it as a pattern of maltreatment sustained over a long period of time, producing a relatively low level of immediate risk. Physical abuse, in contrast, is commonly seen as a critical event, representing high-risk behaviour ... most of the literature on child fatalities caused by maltreatment has dealt with physical abuse. (pp. 309–10)

He reports findings very similar to those of Anderson *at al.* but adds an interesting detail on perpetrator characteristics: 'males accounted for only 15 per cent of the neglect fatalities but were responsible for 57 per cent of the physical abuse deaths' (p. 313).

The problem with the concept of neglect is that, except in its grossest forms it is difficult to define: an act of omission rather than commission. And what parent is constantly vigilant or never takes a risk? As Margolin says: 'In the vast majority of fatalities from neglect, a caregiver was simply not there when needed at a critical moment' (p. 314).

Neglect fatalities are a subset of accidental deaths. Boys are consistently more accident-prone than girls from infancy through to adolescence. Figure 4.9 shows deaths due to injury and

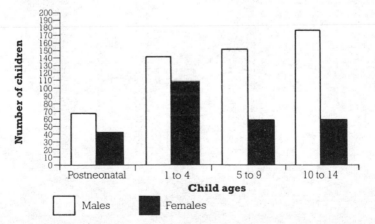

Figure 4.9 Childhood mortality due to injury and poisoning by age-group and gender, England and Wales 1988 (data derived from OPCS, 1991b, Table B, p. xi).

poisoning for both sexes in England and Wales during 1988 (OPCS, 1991b).

It should be noted, however, that deaths in these categories have declined dramatically in children, *especially* boys, over the

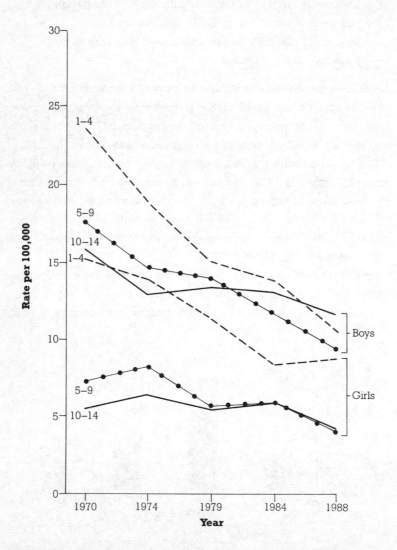

Figure 4.10 Deaths from accidents and violence 1970–88 England and Wales (from OPCS, 1991b, p. xi, Figure C).

past twenty years. It is not clear whether this is due to improved care or improved medical treatment – probably the latter (see Figure 4.10).

We turn finally to an extended consideration of the postneonatal stage where, as we have seen (Figures 4.1 and 4.2), children are most likely to die and where there has been least improvement due, in the main, to the large number of fatalities classified as *Sudden Infant Death*.

THE SUDDEN INFANT DEATH SYNDROME

The 1991 OPCS report dealing with childhood mortality statistics in England and Wales during 1988 has the following paragraph in its introduction:

> The main cause of postneonatal death was sudden infant death syndrome (SIDS, ICD 798.0). Almost one-half of all postneonatal deaths were attributed to SIDS. There were 64 per cent more SIDS among males than females, and even when adjusted to allow for more males being born than females, the male rates were still higher. There are very few sudden deaths with unknown cause (ICD 798) after one year of age; in 1988 there were 26 sudden deaths in children aged one, five deaths to children aged two, and three deaths to children aged three (3 per cent of deaths at ages 1-4, a similar proportion as in previous years). (OPCS, 1991b, p. xi)

The Sudden Infant Death Syndrome is defined as 'the death, unexpected by history, of any infant or young child in whom a thorough post-mortem examination fails to show an adequate cause' (cited by Berger, 1979, p. 554).

SIDS is frequently in the news, usually because there has been a new proposal in the medical literature as to causes which, in fact, remain elusive. Few people, however, realize that the category accounts for such a large proportion of infant deaths.

Since 1988 and up to 1991 there has been a fall of some 35 per cent in these 'cot death' rates in England and Wales (OPCS data cited by Lewis, Samuels and Southall, 1993) and over 40 per cent in Scotland (Gibson, Brooke and Keeling, 1991). There has been much debate in the medical literature as to the reasons for this reduction, e.g. Lewis *et al.* (*op. cit.*). Avoiding overheating, the prone sleeping position, parental smoking, and the reduced risk of respiratory infection through the reduced use of infant welfare clinics have all been suggested. However, Gibson *et al.* (*op. cit.*) caution against the argument that the reductions are directly due to public-health campaigns because the decline in this category is apparent worldwide. It may well be that the high reported level of SIDS deaths in 1988 was artifactual, a consequence of the 'popularity' of this category. The 1992 OPCS publication dealing with social and biological factors relating to perinatal and infant mortality in England and Wales up to 1990 comments in the introduction:

> During the 1970s there was increasing interest in and recognition of SIDS, and mortality rates attributed to this syndrome rose continually, reaching a rate of 2.0 per 1,000 live births in 1988. During the same period, deaths attributed to respiratory diseases (ICD 460–519) fell ... suggesting that there was a transfer of diagnosis to SIDS by certifiers. In contrast, between 1988 and 1990 the numbers of postneonatal deaths due to respiratory diseases fell by 36 per cent (from 318 in 1988 to 204 in 1990) and the numbers attributed to SIDS also fell by 25 per cent (from 1,382 in 1988 to 1,034 in 1990). (OPCS, 1992b, p. xiv)

The diagnosis of SIDS, often described as a 'cot death', carries with it connotations of unexplained *natural* causes. The notion that a proportion of SIDS is due to *infanticide* (murder by the mother) or *filicide* (murder by either of the parents), by means primarily of suffocation, has slowly been gaining recognition over the past decade. This is a most sensitive topic and needs to be considered carefully. But because the SIDS category of infant deaths is so large, its importance is not in question.

SIDS AND CHILD ABUSE

Professor John Emery of the Department of Paediatrics in the University of Sheffield puts SIDS into historical context:

> If we consider the situation of children found unexpectedly dead in their cots and presenting as cot deaths 40 or more years ago, there were many who believed that most of these were instances of filicide. Many parents were submitted to intense interrogation and investigation by the police. As knowledge of paediatric pathology increased it was realised by many that a considerable number of these deaths were due to natural causes, and that many parents were being harassed quite unnecessarily when babies presented in this way. Through social and humanitarian motives a group in Seattle came forward with the concept of there being a sudden infant death syndrome, which is an unexplained natural cause of death. ... Being a condition of unknown aetiology, nobody is to blame or need do anything active about it except to comfort the parents – and many are active here. Against this background the suggestion that some of these babies' deaths are due to filicide becomes unacceptable. ... The development of the concept of SIDS as a natural disease was not based upon any firm evidence, and thus the possibility of most of these deaths being due to filicide remained. But we can now say with much greater certainty than ever before that more than nine out of ten cot deaths are *not* due to filicide ... (Emery, 1985, pp. 506–7)

The situation Emery describes is the familiar 'swing of the pendulum' where the previously dominant explanation becomes unacceptable. A modest movement back in the other direction has been apparent since the late 1970s.

Berger (1979) wrote:

> Before the recognition of SIDS as a discrete entity,
> many parents whose infants were victims of SIDS were
> falsely accused of having killed their infants. In recent
> years there has been increasing emphasis on avoiding
> this error, and many paediatricians no longer consider
> child abuse part of the differential diagnosis when SIDS
> is the suspected diagnosis. This report is prompted by
> two recent examples of child abuse which simulated
> 'near-miss' SIDS. (p. 554)

Berger goes on to describe the cases where infants suffered recurrent episodes of apnoea (breathing stopped) or cyanosis (symptoms of lack of oxygen). The two siblings of one of the infants had died unexpectedly at 6 weeks and $4\frac{1}{2}$ months, with the cause given as SIDS. The episodes only occurred when the mother was present, whether at home or in hospital; in both cases the mothers were found attempting to suffocate the children in hospital.

Berger makes the point that:

> These two examples of child abuse by suffocation
> presenting as near-miss SIDS demonstrate the difficulty
> in differentiating these diagnoses. In both cases the
> initial histories, presentations, physical examinations,
> and laboratory findings were compatible with either
> diagnosis. (p. 555)

Direct clinical evidence of that kind is rare and post-mortem examination is often inconclusive. Emery (1985) comments:

> In detective fiction the forensic pathologist is able to
> say with certainty whether or not a person has died

from asphyxia – in fact this is by no means the case.
The classically accepted stigmata petechiae are known
to have very complicated patterns of causology. We
have all seen children who have been accidentally
suffocated by plastic bags over their faces and who
have shown none of the classic stigmata of suffocation
or asphyxia. (p. 505)

At a clinical case level the trail is difficult to follow and presents unusual routes back to the suspicion surrounding some 'cot deaths'. Meadow (1984) describes 32 cases of fictitious epilepsy in children. This is the so-called 'Munchausen syndrome by proxy' where parents (usually mothers) present their children as suffering from a disorder which is false, sometimes leading to extensive medical investigations. Meadow comments:

The index patients had 33 brothers and sisters. 11 of
these were alive and well, but 9 siblings were similarly
afflicted by false epilepsy, 5 had suffered non-
accidental injury, 7 had died suddenly and
unexpectedly in infancy (cot death), and 1 had
incurred unexplained brain damage. (p. 25)

A report by Southall *et al.* (1987) in the *British Medical Journal* provided incontrovertible evidence in that in two cases where mothers were suspected of inducing apnoeic episodes by smothering, covert video surveillance by nurses and police officers recorded them doing just that. A similar finding had been reported earlier by Rosen *et al.* (1983). Remarkable in both reports was the apparently exemplary behaviour of the mothers involved.

Such unequivocal evidence is rare. Emery (1986) in a letter to the *New England Journal of Medicine* writes:

We have found that infant deaths cannot simply be
divided into the 'explained' and the 'unexplained', but
cover the whole spectrum from the fully explained to
the completely unexplained, with a partial probable

explanation being found in the majority of cases. Throughout our studies we have found that the possibility of accidental suffocation has been raised in approximately 10 per cent of cases, almost always in situations of gross social deprivation, and the possibility of active intervention on the part of one or the other parent has been raised in another 10 per cent of deaths, approximately. (p. 1676)

The link between SIDS and social disadvantage and/or a previous family history of child abuse has been indicated in a number of studies. An early investigation in Oxford by Fedrick (1973) of 206 such cases found 'statistically highly significant correlations ... with low maternal age, high parity [many children], and low social class, the last two associations being more marked among the mothers of infants who died after the 12th week' (p. 93).

Roberts, Lynch and Golding (1980) studied the postneonatal death rate amongst 332 infants from 160 families where child abuse had already been identified. There were nine deaths compared with 2.9 that would have been predicted from legitimacy, social class, age and parity distribution ($p = 0.003$).

Oliver (1983) carried out a longitudinal study of 147 families with a history of multi-agency support through two generations and with a history of child neglect and abuse. In a period of 21 years from 1960 to 1980, 560 children were born to these families; 41 of them died. Nearly two-thirds of these children had died in the postneonatal period, some 26 children in all. The comparable national rate for social class V was 6.3. This ratio bears comparison with the study by Roberts *et al.*

Fatal abuse mainly involves very young children: the physically vulnerable who cannot speak for themselves. The history of the battered child syndrome described in Chapter 2 shows that we are now well aware of the more dramatic signs of maltreatment in infancy, even if we cannot always prevent it. But we are now down to the more subtle forms of child abuse where ascertainment provides very real problems; not least the problem of dealing unjustly with bereaved parents. Detected or not, fatal child abuse is a source of continuing psychological harm to the parent who is driven to commit such an act. For that reason as well as the protection of infants it is necessary to know the true character and scale of the problem.

Because of the problems inherent in obtaining clinical evidence it is likely, at the present, that epidemiological studies will provide the most convincing evidence of an association between SIDS and child abuse. A recent study by Newlands and Emery (1991) in South Derbyshire exemplifies this approach.

Taking all children born between 1 January 1984 and 30 June 1988, whose names appeared on the Child Protection Register as victims of abuse or 'at risk' of abuse (288 in all), they found that one in 30 of these children had a sibling whose death was registered as caused by SIDS. With a local SIDS rate of 3.1:1000, fractionally less than two such deaths would have been predicted. In fact there were nine, giving a rate of 15.6:1000, a highly significant difference. The deaths (average age at death 15.3 weeks) associated with abusing families represented approximately one-tenth of the total 'cot deaths' (9.5 per cent). The authors conclude:

> It is now increasingly recognised that deaths of children registered as SIDS deaths have multiple causalities, and the future lies in breaking down such deaths into different etiological groups ... Among these, filicide should be considered. It is also recognised that it is not possible on purely anatomical grounds to differentiate between classic SIDS and deaths due to asphyxia. We are in no position to conclude that an unexpected child death occurring in an abusing family has been the subject of filicide, but this is a possibility which should be seriously considered in these circumstances. (p. 278)

5

A COMPARISON OF PHYSICAL AND SEXUAL ABUSE

We can most of us understand how, under certain circumstances, parents might physically maltreat their children. Sexual abuse, however, is quite a different matter. Until the early 1980s, society in general found it hard to believe that there was a widespread tendency for caretakers and other adults to exploit children sexually. Even if it were true at all, surely such occurrences were rare, and confined to a small number of seriously disturbed or psychopathic individuals?

Awareness of the problem of child sexual abuse came earlier in the US (see Finkelhor, 1979) and the category was included in the national records maintained by NCCAN from their inception in 1976. Table 5.1 from Russell and Trainor, 1984, shows the progression of child sexual abuse reports from that date. Note that the percentage almost doubles from 1976 to 1977 and is starting to tail off by 1982.

The category of sexual abuse was not generally used on Child Abuse/Protection Registers in the UK until the early 1980s, starting with very low numbers of reports which increased rapidly: a reflection, on a lower scale, of the American experience. The NSPCC study, for example (Creighton, 1992), reports data on sexual abuse only from 1983. Numbers of reports peaked in 1987 (the year of the Cleveland Inquiry) and then started to decline (see Figure 5.1). Creighton comments (p. 60) that the data 'certainly showed evidence of increased caution in the cases of sexual abuse'.

This caution is doubtless justified to some extent (see pages 30 to 33 of Howitt's 1992 book *Child Abuse Errors* for a discussion of the 'false positives' problem).

The 'evidence factor' is a major distinction between sexual and physical abuse. Although evidence of physical injury may under-estimate the level of physical violence towards children (Straus, 1979) it is in direct relation to it. And physical injuries are their own evidence even when the probability of their being 'acci-dental' is hard to evaluate (and even then neglect may be inferred, especially if the 'accidents' are recurrent).

In cases of sexual abuse, medical (i.e. physical) evidence has often disappeared if the examination is more than 72 hours after the incident (Finkel, 1989). And presumed physical signs of anal or vaginal penetration have proved unreliable within a large margin of error (e.g. Emans *et al.*, 1987; McCann *et al.*, 1989). The most reliable evidence of sexual abuse is the child's verbal testimony provided that it is appropriately elicited: a problem in itself (see Gillham, 1992).

Are the kind of children who are physically abused similar to

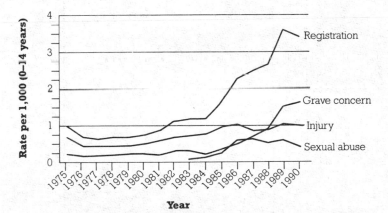

Figure 5.1 Registration, injury, sexual abuse and grave concern rates in England and Wales by year, 1975–90: NSPCC sample (from Creighton, 1992, Figure 7).

Table 5.1 Type of maltreatment by year: all reports (from Russell and Trainor, 1984, p. 94, Table A–IV–1)

	1976 (N = 62.911)	1977 (N = 68.593)	1978 (N = 79.871)	1979 (N = 189.694)	1980 (N = 268.488)	1981 (N = 235.768)	1982 (N = 331.544)
% major physical injury	3.1	3.7	3.5	4.5	3.9	4.1	2.4
% minor or unspecified physical injury	19.4	21.2	21.7	18.5	22.9	23.5	21.5
% sexual maltreatment	3.2	6.0	6.6	6.0	6.8	7.5	6.9
% deprivation of necessities	70.6	64.0	62.9	65.3	60.7	59.4	62.5
% emotional maltreatment	21.6	25.4	23.8	15.4	13.5	11.8	10.0
% other maltreatment	7.6	7.5	7.4	9.2	7.7	11.7	9.2

those who are sexually abused? The answer is that, over-whelmingly, they are neither the same children nor the same kind of children. However, before discussing the differences, we need to consider the extent to which physically abused children are also sexually abused children.

THE SEXUALLY AND PHYSICALLY ABUSED CHILD

Clinical-medical studies of the relationship between physical and sexual abuse, usually by paediatricians with a specialism in the latter, often report a significant although minority overlap. An early study of a clinical population of sexually abused children in the UK found that in 15 per cent of the children there was evidence of physical injury and in 7 per cent a history of previous injury (Mrazek and Bentovim, 1981, pp. 35–49).

Similar results are reported by Hobbs and Wynne (1987, 1990). The specialist interest of these two paediatricians is well known as a result of the publicity associated with the Cleveland Inquiry. In their 1987 paper they reported that one in ten of 337 sexually abused children they examined had also experienced physical abuse. It has to be emphasized that the population of children they saw was filtered professionally because of their known specialist skills, i.e. it was not a 'representative' group. They comment (p. 837) 'there is commonly a long chain of referral, before the child sees a paediatrician'.

The 1990 paper reports the analysis of a much larger, cumulative case study: 'In the four years 1985–88 inclusive we diagnosed physical abuse in 769 children and sexual abuse in 949 children. These totals included 130 children in whom both physical and sexual abuse was diagnosed' (p. 423). Details of the number of children in each category for each year are given in Table 5.2. Note that the numbers in the combined category are included in the single categories.

Of the 130 children, 77 were girls and 53 were boys with mean

Table 5.2 Numbers of physically and sexually abused children by year of diagnosis (from Hobbs and Wynne, 1990, p. 423, Table 1)

Year	Non-accidental injury	Sexual abuse	Non-accidental injury and sexual abuse
1985	182	100	13
1986	207	237	35
1987	207	333	40
1988	173	279	42
Totals	769	949	130

ages of 5.7 and 6.8 years respectively. The authors comment that their data reflect previous reports which found that combined physical and sexual abuse predominantly involves young children. Figure 5.2 from the same study shows the clear tendency for

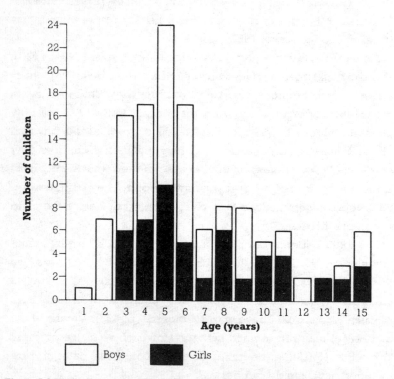

Figure 5.2 Physically and sexually abused children by age and gender at the times of diagnosis (from Hobbs and Wynne, 1990, p. 423, Figure 1).

Table 5.3 Percentage rates of registration during the years 1988–90 inclusive by category: Department of Health and NSPCC data (England) (from Creighton, 1992, p. 13, Table 1A (i))

CATEGORY OF REGISTRATION	1988		1989		1990	
	DofH*	NSPCC	DofH	NSPCC	DofH	NSPCC
Neglect (alone)	11	3	11	9	9	8
Physical abuse (alone)	25	33	24	27	21	28
Sexual abuse (alone)	17	23	14	17	12	15
Emotional abuse (alone)	4	2	4	3	5	2
Grave concern (alone)	40	33	44	41	50	45
Neglect, physical abuse and sexual abuse	–	–	–	–	–	–
Neglect and physical abuse	1	1	2	1	2	1
Neglect and sexual abuse	1	–	–	–	–	–
Physical and sexual abuse	1	–	1	1	1	1
Total registered (100%)	23,000	2,672	26,900	3,592	28,200	3,364

* Year 1 April – 30 March

73

boys to be more susceptible to combined forms of abuse at a younger age.

It is necessary to set against these clinical findings the national statistics collected by the NSPCC and the Department of Health (previously cited in Chapter 3). The percentage category registration rates from both sources are combined in Table 5.3 (from Creighton, 1992).

It can be seen that the category of physical with sexual abuse does not rise above 1 per cent, with *neglect* and sexual abuse hardly registering.

Both kinds of data (clinical and registration reports) no doubt have their own systematic biases. Only a methodologically adequate prevalence study could resolve the discrepancies. What we can say, however, is that the great majority of physically abused children are not also sexually abused.

DIFFERENCES BETWEEN THE TWO GROUPS

Figure 5.3 (from Jason *et al.*, 1982) shows the age distribution of cases of sexual and physical abuse, by age per 100,000 children, confirmed by the Georgia Department of Protective Services. The age distributions are quite different: principally that children under five are the most likely to be physically abused, and children over five the most likely to be sexually abused.

In this study three other main differences between the two groups emerged:

- 91 per cent of the sexually abused group were girls (although this percentage almost certainly underestimates the true proportions of sexually abused boys: see Gillham, 1991, p. 9); the proportions of boys and girls physically abused were approximately equal;
- 98 per cent of the known perpetrators of sexual abuse were male as against 56 per cent of the perpetrators of physical abuse;

74

A Comparison of Physical and Sexual Abuse

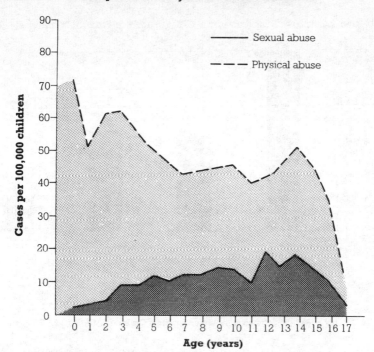

Figure 5.3 Rates by age of victim for confirmed cases of sexual and physical child abuse in Georgia, July – December 1979 (from Jason *et al.*, 1982, p. 3345, Figure 1).

- perpetrators of sexual abuse were more likely to be unknown or unrelated to the child (11 per cent versus 3 per cent), but the actual difference is almost certainly much greater: see the discussion that follows.

Direct comparison can be made between these data and those contained in the NSPCC study (Creighton, 1992):

- 80 per cent of the sexually abused group were girls, and again the proportions of boys and girls physically abused was approximately equal;
- probably only 5 per cent of suspected perpetrators of sexual abuse were female (data not clear in this respect); natural mothers and fathers were equally

75

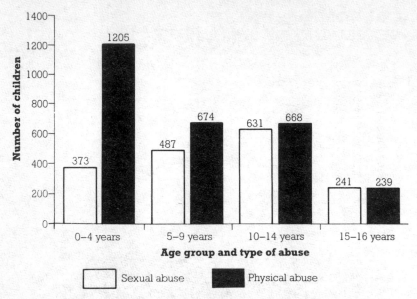

Figure 5.4 Age distribution of registered cases of physical abuse and sexual abuse: NSPCC sample 1988–90 combined (data derived from Creighton, 1992, p. 20, Table 6).

implicated in physical abuse, but substitute fathers more so;

- 15 per cent of perpetrators of sexual abuse were unrelated to the child as against 4 per cent in the case of physical injury.

The age comparison in the NSPCC study is given in Figure 5.4 above and reflects the same overall picture as the American study.

Because sexual abuse is more easily concealed and presents greater problems of evidence, *reported* incidence data are particularly subject to referral bias. The implications of this will now be considered more fully.

THE COMPARATIVE EPIDEMIOLOGY OF SEXUAL AND PHYSICAL ABUSE

Perhaps the most powerful belief, as general amongst professional workers as in the population at large, is that sexual abuse mainly occurs within the family. The strength of this professional assumption was demonstrated in the organization of the *National Study of the Incidence and Severity of Child Abuse and Neglect* conducted in 1979 and 1980, constituting one of the largest and most systematic attempts to collect data on cases of child abuse in the United States. Reviewing this study Finkelhor and Hotaling (1984) comment that:

> The legislation setting up the National Center for Child
> Abuse and Neglect and also mandating the NI study
> chose to define child abuse as acts committed by a
> 'parent substitute or other adult caretakers'. . . .
> Although this is an issue which has been substantially
> debated within the field, it is our own opinion that this
> is a very unfortunate limitation to put on the definition
> of child sexual abuse. *Child sexual abuse differs in this*
> *regard compared to almost all other forms of child abuse*
> *and neglect.* Adults who commit physical assaults or
> emotionally or physically neglect children are almost
> always parents and/or caretakers. Estimates vary, but
> from retrospective reports it seems probable that non-
> family abuse actually constitutes a *majority* of all abuse.
> (p. 26, emphasis added)

Presumably the assumption operating in the legislative programme that Finkelhor and Hotaling criticize was that sexual abuse was some kind of extension of other forms of physical abuse and neglect.

The professional response to child sexual abuse came from a system (in medicine and social work) conditioned by what was known about child physical abuse, i.e. that it was associated with indices of social deprivation and that it occurred, almost exclusively, within the family. There was, therefore, an in-built bias, not just in people's minds but in the way the system operated. The analysis of all US reporting data on child abuse and neglect for the period 1976–82 carried out by the American Humane Association (Russell and Trainor, 1984) casts some light on the operation of this process. For example, over the seven-year period, the percentage of families of sexually abused children receiving public assistance declined from 39.8 to 29.3 per cent, although there was no similar decline in families where other forms of abuse were reported (stable at around 45 per cent). The authors comment (p. 35) that the 'trend perhaps indicates that a new population of sexual abuse families is being identified – one that is less tied to public welfare bureaucracy' and that 'another new population of sexual abuse victims is now being identified – one that is less visible to health professionals . . .'

No such trend is apparent even in much more recent reported incidence data in the UK. Data on the employment and social class status of abusive parents in the NSPCC study (Creighton, 1992) show absolutely no difference in these terms for the two categories of abuse; see Table 5.4.

We know that physical abuse is strongly related to indices of poverty and this is also apparent in the few *prevalence* studies (see p. 38). The research literature on child sexual abuse is different in that there are many more prevalence studies, some more population representative than others, based on retrospective reports by adults of their childhood experiences. It is possible to compare these prevalence studies with reported incidence studies to estimate reporting bias.

The present author carried out an aggregate analysis of published incidence and prevalence studies (Gillham, 1991):

From the figures [in reported studies] it would appear
that the overwhelming proportion of sexual abusers

Table 5.4 Employment of parents by reason for registration 1988–90 combined: NSPCC sample (from Creighton, 1992, p. 29, Table 14)

REASON FOR REGISTRATION	MOTHERS				FATHERS			
	Employed No.	(%)*	Unemployed No.	(%)	Employed No.	(%)*	Unemployed No.	(%)
Physical injury	470	(19)	1506	(59)	887	(43)	771	(37)
Sexual abuse	297	(19)	906	(57)	489	(37)	450	(34)
Neglect	40	(6)	506	(78)	147	(32)	216	(47)
Emotional abuse	24	(11)	167	(75)	66	(39)	86	(51)
Failure to thrive	6	(6)	93	(85)	15	(17)	54	(63)
Neglect and physical abuse	7	(7)	72	(72)	16	(20)	39	(48)
Physical and sexual abuse	4	(7)	40	(71)	15	(37)	16	(39)
Grave concern	372	(10)	2340	(65)	903	(33)	1164	(42)
All registrations	1222	(14)	5640	(64)	2541	(36)	2807	(40)
No information	1945 (22)				1634 (23)			

* Percentages relate to the different numbers of mothers and fathers in the sample when parental situation adjusted for.

are known to their victims and that 'stranger danger' is
not the main threat to children.

The category 'family' used in these studies normally
includes any relation and often includes co-habitees,
etc. 'Acquaintances' are people known to the child but
not related or living as part of the family; 'strangers'
are those unknown to the child. In the 'family' category
the range for these incidence studies is 23.7 to 71 per
cent (average 45 per cent); the range for the
'acquaintances' category is 17 to 58.1 per cent
(average 37.9 per cent); and for 'strangers' the range is
3 to 46.5 per cent (average 17 per cent).

However, when we look at prevalence studies, the
data reveal significant differences ... Here the average
percentage for family abuse is 22.8 per cent (half the
'incidence' average); and while the average for
'acquaintance' abuse is almost exactly the same at 35.8
per cent, for 'stranger' abuse the average is 41.7 per
cent, i.e. more than twice that shown by the incidence
studies. This means that prevalence studies show the
relative proportion of 'family' abusers as opposed
to 'stranger' abusers to be approximately reversed.
(p. 18)

It seems that, counter-intuitively, intrafamilial abuse is more
likely to be detected and reported. Finkelhor (1979) observes:

Parents (mostly fathers and stepfathers) make up a
large proportion of reported cases for several reasons.
For one thing, they are conspicuous, create concern,
and are thus likely to be pursued by those who know
about them until they become official statistics. For
another thing, although many families try to contain
knowledge about parent–child incest, the dynamics
are so volatile and the potential for conflict so great
that they must be harder to hush up permanently than

other kinds of children's sexual abuse. Thus even
though the motivation for silence may be greater, the
actual ability to contain it is less. (p. 140)

When we are dealing with social work/child protection register
statistics, another 'bias' operates in that these agencies see their
work as being with *families*, so that it is predominantly intrafamilial sexual abuse which is referred to them or retained by
them within their system. Cases may not (in some services
explicitly *will* not) be registered if family work is not involved.

Despite these biases the proportion of parents or family
members identified as perpetrators in reported incidence studies
is markedly different from studies of physical abuse. When the
comparison is with *prevalence* studies it is clear that we are
dealing with a largely different set of incidents. One major
difference, then, is at the level of familial involvement.

The other, even more marked difference – again mainly
apparent from *prevalence* studies of sexual abuse – is in the social
class membership of the victims (and presumably the abusers).

As we have seen in Chapter 3 both the victims and perpetrators
of physical abuse are predominantly from the socially disadvantaged sections of the community. From the NSPCC studies it
would *appear* that this is also the case with sexual abuse (refer
back to Table 5.4). But when prevalence studies of sexual abuse
are analysed it is clear that this form of abuse is almost exactly
evenly distributed across *all* social classes. The implications of
this discrepancy are extensive.

Reviewing the main American studies Finkelhor (1987) comments that they have:

provided information about the distribution of sexual
abuse within various sociodemographic subgroups in
the communities studied. *Interestingly, the studies are
fairly uniform in failing to find differences in rates
according to social class or racial subdivision.* (p. 234,
emphasis added)

Table 5.5 Demographic comparison of respondents with the general population (from Baker and Duncan, 1985, p. 460, Table 1)

	Total No.	Sex		Age							Class					Area		
		M %	F %	15–24 %	25–34 %	35–44 %	45–54 %	55–64 %	65+ %	AB %	C1 %	C2 %	DE %	Urban %	Mixed %	Rural %
General population	2019	48	52	19	19	19	14	13	16	16	22	33	29	57	27	16
Abused group	206	40	60	25	19	24	15	11	5	13	27	34	26	57	24	19
Non-abused group	1553	48	52	18	20	17	14	13	17	16	21	33	30	57	27	16
Refused to answer	259	52	48	19	13	22	12	14	19	16	24	32	29	57	30	13

Precise information on this point for the UK is provided by Baker and Duncan (1985) who analysed data obtained from a representative quota sample of 2,019 men and women aged 15 years and over who were interviewed as part of a MORI survey. Ten per cent reported that they had been sexually abused before the age of 16 (12 per cent of females; 8 per cent of males).

They report that there were: 'no significant differences between the abused, non-abused and refused-to-answer groups with regard to social class and area of residence, and all are distributed in proportion' (p. 459). Table 5.5 from their study summarizes their findings.

Classes A/B/C1 are non-manual; C2/D/E are manual. Of the abused group 40 per cent are in the former, 60 per cent are in the latter – almost identical with the population at large. Compare this with the social class pattern of reported and registered cases in the NSPCC study discussed on p. 30.

The implications of this difference for the workings of our child-protection system are profound; clearly the present system does not serve to protect middle-class victims of sexual abuse.

In summary, physical abuse can be seen as partly a response to the stresses of poverty, part of a failure to cope. Sexual abuse *may* occur for the same reasons but in general it would seem to have a different dynamic, to involve different populations of children and abusers.

6
THE CAUSES OF CHILD ABUSE

That parents should injure young and defenceless children is no longer incredible; the past thirty years have given us a better appreciation of the stresses of parenting. But the formulation and reformulation of the problem has been a lengthy process.

The history of attempts to understand child maltreatment is an object lesson in the difficulties of arriving at an adequate explanation of complex social behaviour: one emphasis has succeeded another. The successive paradigms can most simply be described as *psychiatric*, emphasizing the pathological individual histories and personalities of abusing parents; *sociological*, emphasizing the socioeconomic and demographic factors that are likely to increase parental stress; and the *ecological*, which emphasizes the interaction between individual dispositions and environmental factors.

This is a simplification, but the shifts in explanatory emphasis over three decades have been marked, and are readily discerned in the literature.

Kempe *et al.* (1962) in their historic paper stated:

> Psychiatric factors are probably of prime importance
> in the pathogenesis of the disorder, but our knowledge
> of these factors is limited. Parents who inflict abuse on
> their children do not necessarily have psychopathic or
> sociopathic personalities or come from borderline
> socioeconomic groups, although most published cases
> have been in these categories. In most cases some

defect in character structure is probably present; often
parents may be repeating the type of child care
practised on them in their childhood. (p. 24)

The latter notion of the direct intergenerational transmission of
abusive behaviour has been a most potent myth, having some
foundation in fact and being simple and powerful as an explanation. It is interesting to note that in the past decade such an
explanation has been promoted to explain child sexual abuse (see
discussion in Gillham, 1991, p. 69). In the same way that child
molesters report above-average histories of child sexual abuse
(e.g. Groth *et al.*, 1978), so abusing parents may report higher
than average histories of physical abuse. National statistics in the
US based on 13,000 cases give 20.1 per cent of the parents
reporting a history of child abuse (cited in Kadushin and Martin,
1981, p. 20). This issue is discussed more fully in Chapter 7.

The psychodynamic literature on the personality characteristics
of abusive parents is extensive. An empirical study based on
interviews and clinical judgments by Green, Gaines and Sandgrund (1974) is typical in its conclusions and more systematic than
most. They interviewed the mothers or maternal caretakers *only* of
60 physically abused children and claimed to find six personality
characteristics common to most of them:

- a reliance on the child to satisfy dependency needs
  not fulfilled in the relationship with their partner and
  family;
- poor impulse control;
- poor self-concept;
- disturbances of identity;
- projection and externalization of blame to defend
  against feelings of worthlessness;
- misperception of the child.

These probably have some descriptive validity; whether they
can be seen as fundamentally 'causal' is another matter. The

authors use their evidence to provide a characteristically psycho-analytic explanation, as follows:

- the child's nurturant demands intensify the mother's own unsatisfied dependency feelings;
- lacking gratification from her partner she turns to the child for satisfaction of these needs and is frustrated;
- she then unconsciously equates the child with her own critical, rejecting mother because she experiences again the rejection of her childhood;
- the intolerable anxiety, guilt and sense of worthlessness are displaced on to the child via the defence mechanisms of denial and projection;
- she identifies with her mother, representing her punitive superego and attacks the child who symbolizes her past and present inadequacies.

It should be noted that this explanation applies only to maternal abuse. As we have seen in Chapter 3 there are differences in the pattern of abuse by male and female caretakers.

It is not the purpose of this chapter to debunk intraindividual explanations. We can recognize that, leaving aside psychoanalytic notions, something has to happen to how parents feel about and perceive their children for them to become abusers. But the observed 'personality' of abusers may, to a greater or lesser extent, reflect or mediate current social and environmental effects on them.

At this point it may be instructive to consider the changes that have taken place in personality theory over the past twenty-five years. Up to the mid-1960s at least, people's 'personalities' were seen as a cluster of *traits* which, if they changed to some extent in their developmental history, were relatively stable at any one point in time. The pattern of traits varied between individuals but some traits were usually seen as dominant so that it was possible to classify people in terms of a personality typology (e.g. Cattell, 1965). The whole edifice of personality testing was built round the assumption of stable (and measurable) traits. In the late 1960s, however, two major empirical reviews (Vernon, 1964; Mischel, 1968) cast doubts on these theories, especially in relation to the validity of tests that were supposed to measure personality traits. These authors found that tests that were presumed to measure the same traits did not correlate significantly, i.e. there was a lack of *construct* validity, and, more importantly, often did not correlate with real-life observations, i.e. *criterial* validity. As sometimes happens in psychology the pendulum swung strongly the other way so that 'situationism' became a dominant emphasis: such that Pervin (1978) wrote a paper entitled 'Am I me or am I the situation?' His sensible conclusion was as follows:

> The trait ... is a summary concept held to be useful in explaining the consistency that is found in behavior. On the other hand, recognition of the importance of the situation was necessary to explain the inconsistency or variability of behavior. (p. 17)

What we are left with from this controversy is a clear appreciation of two things:

1 A person's characteristics whether 'stable' or not are not sufficient to *explain* his behaviour; they themselves have to be explained;

2 Whatever a person's disposition or tendencies may be, for him to behave in a particular way requires other situational and social components.

Although we may accept this intellectually, it runs counter to our intuitions in a real-life instance. Human actions are committed by human beings not by 'situations' or 'environments'. It is sometimes compelling to believe that people do things because they are 'like that'; it is much harder to believe that given very different circumstances they might be very different people. And even harder to credit that, in any conceivable circumstances we ourselves might be 'like that'.

In the case of child maltreatment the 'situational' emphasis can only be justified if the social and economic circumstances of abusers are, in the main, radically different from non-abusers. What is notable in the literature of the late 1960s and early 1970s is a reluctance to accept the evidence that severe child abuse and neglect is strongly related to socioeconomic status and outright poverty.

It is quite possible that moderate levels of abuse might be differentially interpreted along social class lines and, indeed, there is some evidence that this is so (Newberger *et al.*, 1977; O'Toole *et al.*, 1983) but the resistance to accepting the strong social class association is remarkable and persists to this day.

Pelton (1978) in a paper entitled 'Child abuse and neglect: The myth of classlessness' suggests two main reasons for the maintenance of the myth:

- [It] permits many professionals to view child abuse and neglect as psychodynamic problems, in the context of a medical model of 'disease', 'treatment' and 'cure', rather than as predominantly sociological and poverty-related problems. (pp. 612–13)
- Well-meaning mental health professionals may be drawn to the myth of classlessness, believing that the association of child abuse and neglect with poverty constitutes one more insulting and discriminatory act toward poor people, one more way to 'stigmatize' them unjustly. In fact, the myth does a dis-service to poor people and to the victims of child abuse and neglect; it undermines development of effective approaches to dealing with their real and difficult problems, and directs us toward remedies more oriented to the middle classes. (p. 614)

The argument *for* the relative classlessness of abuse and neglect is essentially that the reporting of cases is selective, that poor families are more subject to public scrutiny and are less likely to have their explanations believed. Whilst these factors probably

have some weight, they cannot account for the extren
of the data.

Physical abuse in its severe forms has 'high visibility'.
from sexual abuse which is largely 'invisible' in its effe
where, incidentally, there is good evidence of a significant, class-
related reporting bias (see Gillham, 1991, p. 28).

Discussing what he calls the 'public scrutiny' argument, Pelton
(*op. cit.*) advances three counter-arguments:

- First, while it is generally acknowledged that greater
  public awareness and new reporting laws have led to
  a significant increase in reporting over the past few
  years, the socioeconomic pattern of these reports has
  not changed appreciably.
- Second [it] cannot explain why child abuse and
  neglect are related to *degrees* of poverty, even *within*
  the same lower class that is acknowledged to be
  more open to public scrutiny.
- Third [it] cannot explain why, among the reported
  cases, the most severe injuries have occurred within
  the poorest families. (pp. 610–11)

Pelton's concluding argument is strongly environmentalist:

... the strong relationship between poverty and child
abuse and neglect suggests that remediation of
situational defects should take precedence over
psychological treatments. These parents' behavior
problems are less likely to be symptoms of
unconscious or intrapsychic conflicts than of concrete
antecedent environmental conditions, crises, and
catastrophes. It is these root causes that must be
addressed. (p. 616)

If the prevention of child abuse depends upon the elimination of
poverty then the prospects do not look very good. No one can
doubt that low income contributes to the stresses of parenting. It
may be one of the necessary conditions but it is clearly not

sufficient. Most poor parents do not abuse their children and it is unlikely that their sole advantage is that they are possessed of a stronger character. The causal pattern is more complex than that.

What are the social, environmental and socioeconomic factors that increase the risk of child abuse, or insure against it?

A first step is to ask: where is child abuse to be found?

Figure 6.1 shows the geographical mapping of all cases of child abuse and neglect in an inner London borough between January 1982 and September 1985 (Cotterill, 1988). Almost all were cases of physical abuse; concentrations in certain areas can clearly be seen.

Cotterill comments:

• household with 1 or more children registered on the child abuse register

Figure 6.1 Geographical mapping of all registered child abuse and neglect in an inner London borough between January 1982 and September 1985 (from Cotterill, 1988, p. 463, Figure 1).

[Figure 6.1] was examined for target areas, being
defined arbitrarily as five or more households with a
registered case of child abuse, in close proximity.
Sixteen target areas were identified: the mean number
of households per target area was 13.5 ± 7 (2 SD),
range 7–20. These 16 areas contained 73% of the cases
registered over the study period. The areas were of
small size, none larger than half a mile across. Of the 16
areas, 12 were housing estates. (p. 466)

Noting the failure of socioeconomic indices in his study to
predict accurately where child abuse would occur, Cotterill
observes that this agrees with the findings of the American
researcher, Garbarino, that child abuse is not predicted solely by
socioeconomic deprivation.

The series of studies carried out by Garbarino and his associates in the 1970s will be considered in some detail because they
were influential in bringing about a major shift in the perception of
child abuse. A key paper, published in 1977 and entitled 'The
human ecology of child maltreatment; A conceptual model for
research' (Garbarino, 1977), provides us with our starting point:

From its beginning as a field of inquiry, child abuse has
been dominated by the clinically defined aura of
pathology that surrounds it. ... professionals and
public alike have defined child abuse as *qualitatively*
different from normal caregiver-child relations. This
'medical model', which concentrates on 'kinds of
people' theories, parallels the early history of research
and theory dealing with juvenile delinquency ... and
in many ways represents a paradigmatic response to
deviance. (p. 721)

He concludes that:

The view that child abuse is best understood as a point
along a more general continuum of caregiver-child

91

relations and only *quantitatively* different from non-abusive relationships has been (and continues to be) a minority position. (p. 722)

It is difficult for us to accept this when we read horrific accounts of extreme forms of abuse: burning and mutilating young children, throwing a baby across a room, and so on ... But once you start to widen the definition of 'abuse', the closer it gets to what might be regarded as 'normal' parenting. It is probable that few of us have not hit our children harder than was necessary in any rational scheme of things, for a variety of reasons but usually to do with the pressures we were under at that particular time.

Garbarino argues that:

> Almost no-one is immune to the *role* of child abuser if
> the discrepancy between situational demands (e.g.
> difficulty of the child, emotional stress on the
> caregiver, etc.) is great enough, although people vary
> in the degree to which they are 'prone' to act in an
> abusive manner. (p. 723)

Garbarino suggests that an 'ecological' approach can cope with the complex interdependence of human systems in producing maltreatment. Drawing on the work of Bronfenbrenner (1977) he characterizes the approach in these ways:

- it focuses on the progressive, mutual adaptation of the individual and the environment;
- it conceives of the environment as an interacting set of systems nested within each other;
- it focuses on the issue of 'social habitability': the question of environmental quality;
- it asserts the need to consider political, economic and demographic factors in shaping the quality of life for individuals.

Garbarino makes the important distinction between the *sufficient* and *necessary* conditions for child abuse to occur, observing that 'the absence of required necessary conditions effectively "disarms" the sufficient conditions' (p. 725). He suggests that there are *two* necessary conditions and that both are best understood within an ecological framework:

- First, for child abuse to occur within family microsystems there must be cultural justification for the use of force against children. (p. 725)
- Of equal or greater importance on a day-to-day basis ... is *isolation from potent support systems.* (p. 726)

The empirical support for this latter assertion comes in two major papers (Garbarino and Crouter, 1978; Garbarino and Sherman, 1980).

Garbarino and Crouter, acknowledging the role of socioeconomic and demographic variables, focus on those interpersonal supports that 'play an important role in mediating the effects of broad socioeconomic, demographic and economic forces on the quality of life for children' (p. 605). Emphasizing the contribution of multivariate techniques of analysis they develop the finding of Garbarino's (1976) study in New York State that 'the degree to which mothers ... are subjected to socioeconomic stress, *without adequate support systems*, accounts for a substantial proportion of the variance in rates of maltreatment' (p. 607).

It is worth noting at this point that Brown and Harris (1978), in an epidemiological study of depression in women, found that interpersonal supports (close relationships) were a major protection against the onset of depressive illness in the face of stressful life events.

Citing the finding of Gray *et al.* (1977) that child maltreatment *and child accidents* decreased when families identified as 'high risk' for maltreatment were involved in long-term support systems they assert that '*child maltreatment is an indicator of the overall quality of life for children and families*' (p. 607, emphasis in original). They go on to argue that family-support systems provide feedback to families, and thus protection for children.

This last point is an important one and reflects Garbarino's (1977) observation that 'child abuse "feeds" on privacy' (p. 727) and Caplan's (1974) notion of social support systems acting as regulators in that they tell the individual 'what is expected of him and guide him in what to do. They watch what he does and they judge his performance' (p. 605).

In their study they examined the effects of a range of socio-economic, demographic and social-support variables. The overwhelming significance of the first two is confirmed, as is the additional importance of the latter. But their analysis leaves plenty of room for individual factors and they note (p. 613) 'the temptations of the "ecological fallacy" (i.e. inappropriately drawing conclusions about individuals based on aggregate data)'.

There are problems with an analysis based on multiple regression techniques as employed in the paper just described. The factors that go in first soak up most of the variance (economic and demographic factors in the study cited) because they are *correlated* with other contributory factors, so making them appear more minor than is in fact the case. An appropriate weighting of each contributory cause is, therefore, difficult to achieve.

Garbarino and Sherman (1980) tackled the problem in a different way, comparing a pair of environments matched for socioeconomic level, but one 'high risk', the other 'low risk' for abuse and neglect.

Accepting that 'child maltreatment is concentrated among socially, economically and psychologically "high risk" families' (p. 188), they argue that this is not the whole story and that we also have to examine 'high risk' environments. They comment (p. 189), 'Families both shape their environments and are shaped by them.'

What emerges from their analysis is that families 'who need the most tend to be clustered together in settings that must struggle to meet their needs' (p. 194). 'Is it neighborhood characteristics that influence family functioning, or do well versus poorly functioning families drift toward high- or low-risk neighborhoods? Our own evidence, and the evidence of others, says "both"' (p. 196).

They conclude: 'we have the repeated finding that ecological niches can "make or break" risky families' (p. 196).

The emphasis of Garbarino and his associates on social support systems represents an important contribution to our understanding of the complex phenomenon of child maltreatment, although it is not without its critics (e.g. Seagull, 1987).

Belsky (1980), however, proposes a more comprehensive theoretical integration which has achieved definitive status, drawing on the work of Tinbergen (1951) and Bronfenbrenner (1977). He argues that 'much of the theoretical conflict that has characterised the study of child maltreatment is more apparent than real' and proposes an *ecological* integration which:

> conceptualizes child maltreatment as a social-psychological phenomenon that is multiply determined by forces at work in the individual (ontogenetic development) and the family (the microsystem), as well as in the community (the exosystem) and the culture (the macrosystem) in which both the individual and the family are embedded. (p. 320)

He emphasizes the importance of 'the individual differences that parents bring with them to the primary microsystem in which their children develop (i.e. the family)' (p. 321).

Without resurrecting the notion that abusive parents were *necessarily* themselves abused he does argue that experience of maltreatment in a general sense, the lack of a loving relationship, may predispose them to respond to certain situations in aggressive and insensitive ways.

He also directs our attention to the *individual characteristics of children* as an element in the predisposition to abuse. He traces this back to the repeated finding that often just one child in a family is singled out for abuse, and the even subtler finding that a disproportionate number of mistreated children were born prematurely. Babies vary in their attractiveness, amenability, feeding

95

Table 6.1 The causes of child maltreatment (from Kaufman and Zigler, 1992, p. 270, Table 12.1. © John Wiley 1992. Reprinted with permission)

Ontogenetic factors	Microsystem factors	Exosystem factors	Macrosystem factors
Risk factors			
History of abuse Alcohol abuse Stressful experiences Low IQ Psychiatric and physical illnesses	Marital discord Single parenthood Premature or unhealthy child	Inadequate health care facilities Social isolation Unsafe neighborhood	Economic recession Cultural acceptance of corporal punishment View of children as possessions
Protective factors			
History of a positive relationship with at least one caregiver Good interpersonal skills High IQ	Supportive spouse Economic security Grandmother or other adult in home to assist with child care	Good community social and health services Affordable quality day care Strong informal social supports Respite care facilities	Economic prosperity Culture opposed to violence Culture opposed to the use of corporal punishment

and sleeping habits and their irritability. Babies who cry persistently are a major problem for their caretakers. Douglas (1989), a clinical psychologist, in a book on behaviour problems in young children devotes a chapter to 'crying babies' and makes the following interesting observations:

> Children of low birthweight are reported to cry more than normal birthweight babies (Butler and Golding, 1986) and a significant difference in the type of cry can differentiate premature babies from healthy full-term babies. Their cries are shorter and more high-pitched (Wasz-Hockert *et al.*, 1985). In a study where parents were shown videos of premature and full-term babies crying, they reported greater autonomic arousal and more negative emotions to the cry of the premature baby (Frodi *et al.*, 1978). *It could be that the more aversive a baby's cries are the less parents can tolerate it and start to feel increasingly stressed and upset.* (p. 178, emphasis added)

The definitive status of Belsky's paper is such that it should be read as a complement to the present chapter. At the same time the past decade has seen significant progress in the unravelling of the complex aetiology of child maltreatment.

Cicchetti and Rizley (1981) argued that a complete account of the aetiology of child maltreatment should include both risk and *protective* factors – the former *increasing* the likelihood of abuse, the latter *decreasing* it. Although protective factors are implied in Belsky's model they are not spelt out.

Kaufman and Zigler (1992), keeping to Belsky's framework, produced the summary table opposite (Table 6.1).

This summarizes the state of knowledge very accessibly; and gives us room to consider those factors we could hope to change, and those we cannot. 'Risk' and 'protective' factors also have to be evaluated from the perspective of the *effects* of abuse on children: this we do in the next chapter.

7

THE PSYCHOLOGICAL EFFECTS OF PHYSICAL ABUSE

Although the effects of some forms of non-accidental injury are lasting (it is, for example, a significant cause of blindness in children) young bodies heal very quickly and there are dramatic 'before and after' photographs in the literature (see Kempe and Helfer, 1980). But what about psychological injury? Does that heal or are there enduring scars, long-lasting emotional impairment?

Writing as recently as 1984, Aber and Cicchetti comment:

> The thought of a maltreated child conjures up images
> of bruises, fractures, malnutrition, and the like. But it is
> the emotional damage, not the physical damage that
> ... may have the most frequent, long-term deleterious
> effect on the development of maltreated children ... It
> is curious then that ... the issue of the impact of
> maltreatment on a child's socio-emotional
> development took so long to interest researchers.
> (p. 147)

The issue of long-term psychological effects cannot be a simple one. The model of main cause-and-effect explanations does not fit the complexity of the problem, even though some such notions are much promoted – in particular the 'intergenerational' hypothesis: the assumption that abused children become abusing parents (or that abusing parents had necessarily been abused themselves).

The real psychological complexity is well-summarized by Cicchetti and Rizley (1981):

> ... there is no specific single pattern that could be described as the profile of abuse or neglect ... Indeed, it would be surprising were any specific pattern to emerge. Children of different ages, at different developmental stages, from diverse environments, and with differing experiences who are exposed to vastly different forms of maltreatment, are likely to manifest vulnerabilities and disabilities in a wide variety of specific, age-appropriate ways. (p. 38)

However, one should not underestimate the pervasiveness of powerfully simple explanations. The embedded character of 'abused becomes abuser' is noted by Kaufman and Zigler (1987):

> The belief that abused children are likely to become abusive parents is widely accepted by professionals and lay people alike. It is noted in introductory psychology textbooks, and advanced on radio and television commercials ... Despite the popularity of this belief, there is a paucity of empirical evidence ... (p. 186)

Kaufman and Zigler (*op. cit.*) demonstrate how research design affects the degree of association between the experience of being abused and becoming an abuser. In particular they emphasize the difference between *prospective* studies where adults, abused as children, are followed up to see if they become abusers, and *retrospective* designs where abusing parents are asked if they were abused as children.

Kaufman and Zigler reviewed ten studies which had compared groups of abusing parents with groups of non-abusing parents. More of the abusing parents reported a history of abuse, but there was usually considerable overlap between the two groups: in other words many parents who do not report a history of abuse in childhood become abusers and a sizeable proportion of parents who were so maltreated, do not. In the studies reviewed (varying greatly in rigour and design) the rate of 'intergenerational transmission' varied from 18 per cent to 70 per cent.

The study with the *lowest* rate (18 per cent) was one that used a prospective rather than a retrospective design. These different approaches produce quite different results. Because the population base rate of abuse is low (most parents do *not* abuse their children) a study which compares similar numbers of abusing and non-abusing parents, even if 'matched' for age, social circumstances, and so on, is bound to miss most non-abusing parents who were abused as children. Only a *prospective* study can overcome that problem.

An example of a prospective study is that of Hunter and Kilstrom (1979). They interviewed 282 parents of newborn babies and followed them up for one year, checking on cases of neglect or abuse registered in the state central agency. At the initial interview 49 parents reported a childhood history of abuse or neglect. At the follow-up, ten babies were reportedly maltreated: nine of them had parents with a history of abuse or neglect. This is a highly significant overlap, but the fact remains that 40 parents with a history of abuse and neglect were *not* identified as maltreaters.

Commenting on this study Kaufman and Zigler point out that it:

> ... illustrates how variations in the choice of subjects
> (identified abusers *vs* high-risk sample) and
> experimental design (retrospective *vs* prospective)
> affect the outcome of research findings. If this study
> had been conducted retrospectively with only the
> parents who were identified as maltreaters, the link
> between a history of abuse and subsequent child
> abuse would have appeared deceptively strong, since
> nine out of ten of the abusive parents reported a history
> of maltreatment (90%). By employing a prospective

research design, Hunter and Kilstrom were able to identify 40 parents who broke the cycle of abuse (82%). (p. 188)

Other follow-up studies cited by Kaufman and Zigler (e.g. Egeland and Jacobvitz, 1984) report higher rates but involve high-risk groups (low income single parents) where 'the influence of a history of abuse upon subsequent parenting cannot be separated from the effects of poverty, stress and social isolation' (p. 189).

Aggregating the studies Kaufman and Zigler suggest that the best estimate of the rate of intergenerational transmission appears to be 30 per cent ± 5 per cent. They point out that:

> [This] is approximately six times higher than the base rate for abuse in the general population (5%) ... being maltreated as a child is an important risk factor in the etiology of abuse ... [but] many mediating factors affect the likelihood of transmission ... Researchers [should] cease asking, 'Do abused children become abusive parents?' and ask, instead, 'Under what conditions is the transmission of abuse most likely to occur?' (p. 190–1)

ABUSED CHILDREN: THE SEARCH FOR PSYCHOLOGICAL CHARACTERISTICS

Clinical research, often not employing comparison groups, has focused on descriptions of emotional and behavioural disorders supposedly characteristic of a history of abuse. There is no doubt that such children display more disorder. It is equally clear that these diagnostic signs are heterogeneous and non-specific in the main.

Martin and his colleagues at the University of Colorado Medical Center have been foremost in this area of research (e.g. Martin and Beezley, 1977). In a study of 50 abused children ranging in age from 22 months to 13 years they identified *nine* characteristics in varying proportions of these children (*op. cit.*, p. 19):

- impaired ability for enjoyment (33/50);
- behavioural symptoms (e.g. enuresis, aggression, 'inappropriate' behaviour) (31/50);
- low self-esteem (26/50);
- withdrawal (12/50);
- oppositional behaviour (aggressive/non-co-operative) (12/50);
- 'hypervigilance' (wariness, mistrust) (11/50);
- compulsivity ('obsessional' behaviour) (11/50);
- precocious 'pseudoadult' behaviour (10/50);
- school learning problems (9/50).

This reads like a fairly complete list of possible social-emotional disorders in children.

In a review paper, Farber and Egeland (1987) comment:

> The conclusion based on the results from various investigations is that abused children display a wide range of social, emotional, and intellectual problems, and that these exceed the number of problems of nonabused children. There is no consistent or typical personality profile of abused children. (p. 254)

However, amongst this heterogeneity is widespread agreement of consistently higher levels of aggression in abused children. This has been true from the earliest clinical/descriptive reports onwards (e.g. Elmer, 1967; Johnson and Morse, 1968). In a controlled comparison study Reidy (1977) looked at the aggressive characteristics of 20 physically abused, 16 non-abused but neglected and 22 non-maltreated children; average ages of the groups were $6\frac{1}{2}$ to 7 years. Abused children displayed more fantasy aggression in projective tests and very much more overt aggression in play situations; interestingly in the latter context, neglected and non-abused children displayed hardly any aggressive behaviour.

Herrenkohl and Herrenkohl (1981) examined the coping strategies employed by maltreating and non-maltreating families with children in the age-range 18–71 months. There were four groups of families:

- 72 families with at least one maltreated child;
- 72 non-maltreating families receiving welfare support;
- 50 families receiving 'Head Start' (compensatory education) support;
- 50 families served by day-care programmes.

One part of the study involved observing the children in free-play situations. Maltreated children were significantly more aggressive with their peers than children in the other three groups – chiefly in response to difficult tasks or 'interference' by their peers.

The two studies cited are samples of many with similar findings. The danger lies in over-generalization from the consistent trend. In the same way that parents with a history of abuse in childhood *are* more likely to maltreat their children, so are maltreated children more likely to be aggressive. But most individuals avoid this apparent 'causal' pattern; and even where it is true there is more to the outcome than heightened aggressive or abusive tendencies.

Behaviour is not simply caused nor do 'causes' necessarily have simple effects. The consequences of abuse are *mediated*: filtered and changed through the child's own reactivity and by the kinds of help and understanding he or she is given. The effect of how someone behaves towards us depends, for example, on what we take it to *mean*.

Both a child's understanding of its experiences and its reaction to them, emotional or behavioural, change as it grows older. Kagan (1971) makes an important distinction between *heterotypical* and *homotypical* continuity of behaviour. In heterotypical continuity *different* behaviours subserve the same emotional need or trait (e.g. attention, security, mistrust of others); in homotypical continuity the same kinds of behaviour are apparent which may (or may not) serve the same kind of emotional purposes. In other words continuity (and continuity of effects) is not always apparent on the surface.

Changes in the child are part of a developing *transaction* between the child and its caretakers (particularly the mother). Each affects the behaviour and feelings and understanding of the other: within an environment that affects them both. This developmental-interaction perspective is exemplified in the research of Egeland detailed below (Farber and Egeland, 1987).

THE MINNESOTA MOTHER–CHILD INTERACTION PROJECT

This prospective longitudinal study followed up a group of mothers considered at risk for abuse and neglect. Enrolled in the study *prior* to the birth of their first child were 267 women: all were of low socioeconomic status, most in receipt of welfare benefit. The average age was 20.5 years and 62 per cent of them were single.

Assessment of the children and their mothers began shortly after birth. The children were assessed on quality of attachment to their mother at 12 months and 18 months and the competence of their approach to tasks at the 24 months, 42 months and immediately preschool level.

From the total sample four 'maltreatment' groups were identified:

- physically abusive mothers
- hostile/verbally abusive mothers
- psychologically unavailable mothers
- neglectful mothers

A control group of mothers who clearly provided adequate care was also chosen from the at-risk sample.

Farber and Egeland (*op. cit.*) describe the characteristics of the maltreating mothers as follows:

> Behavior of mothers in the physically abusive group ranged from frequent and intense spanking while disciplining their children to unprovoked, angry outbursts resulting in serious injury, such as cigarette burns. The mothers in the hostile/verbally abusive group chronically found fault with their children and criticized them in an overly harsh fashion. The difference between these mothers and the physically abusive mothers was in the chronic nature of their abuse; they continually berated their children.
>
> The psychologically unavailable group consisted of detached, emotionally uninvolved mothers. They showed a lack of emotional responsiveness to their children and interacted only when necessary. They seldom would comfort or console the children when the children were distressed, nor would they respond to the children's attempts to elicit positive social interactions. These women appeared depressed and withdrawn.
>
> Mothers in the neglectful group were irresponsible in managing the day-to-day activities of child rearing. They failed to provide the necessary physical and health care for their children and did not protect them from possible dangers in the home. ...
>
> Although there was overlap among the groups the purpose of trying to delineate four groups was to determine whether specific patterns of maltreatment resulted in specific developmental consequences.
> (pp. 263–4)

'Anxious' attachment was noted in a significantly larger proportion of children in the maltreatment groups at 18 months but it was noted in *all* those whose mothers were in the 'psychologically unavailable' group. Children in the 'physically abused' group were generally less competent at later ages up to preschool; the effects of verbal abuse were less consistent. Neglected children seemed the most unhappy and the least positive and organized in their response. The investigators note however:

> children of psychologically unavailable mothers
> exhibited the largest number of pathological
> behaviors ... and ... displayed progressively more
> maladaptive development at each period of
> assessment. The major decline in functioning between
> 12 months and preschool indicates that the caretakers'
> lack of emotional responsiveness is a devastating form
> of abuse. (p. 266)

On the other side Farber and Egeland point to the significance of some positive outcomes in the abused group: *some* abused children were securely attached to their mothers *and* competent at later ages. They relate this to family living patterns:

> The family living patterns were highly related to the
> attachment outcomes. In the intact families, 72% of the
> abused infants were *securely* attached ... Conversely,
> in the one-parent families 67% were *anxiously* attached
> ... Mothers of securely attached abused children
> received more emotional support than did mothers of
> anxiously attached infants. (p. 271, emphasis added)

The authors conclude by emphasizing the importance of the study of *resilience*:

> Environmental variables were more important than
> constitutional variables. Two of the most important
> environmental factors were the presence of a male
> partner in the home and the mother's emotional
> support for the child. ... In general, even though the
> children were maltreated, they were more likely to be
> competent where there was some indication of

maternal interest in them and where the mothers were able to respond to them emotionally. . . .

Our hope behind invulnerability research is that, by studying the good outcomes along with the bad, investigators may find factors that will be useful in prevention and/or intervention. *The results of our study indicate that resources for prevention should be directed toward helping at-risk mothers in the first year of life.* (pp. 284–5, emphasis added)

THE 'INVULNERABLE' CHILD

The notion of 'invulnerability' or 'resilience' relates to the differential effects of maltreatment, which also raises the question of the *direction* of effects. Are maltreated and neglected infants so treated because they are in some way difficult or unsatisfactory or do they become so as a *consequence* of their treatment? Some congenital conditions such as low birth weight, prematurity and birth complications have been found more often in the histories of abused children (e.g. Hunter *et al.*, 1978) but this is not a general finding (e.g. Starr, 1982), a problem being that these conditions are correlated with social disadvantage which itself predisposes to neglect and maltreatment. Infants maltreated later in the first year of life have variously been reported as difficult, unco-operative, whiny and clinging and there is more general agreement here (e.g. Johnson and Morse, 1968; George and Main, 1979).

Crittenden (1985) carried out a longitudinal intervention study which sheds some light on these issues. A total of 73 mother–infant pairs were studied, all of whom were of low socioeconomic status and receiving welfare support. Of the group, 17 had been classified as abusing, 21 as neglecting and 22 as 'problematic', the other 13 presumably functioning adequately. There were no significant differences between the groups in the congenital conditions of the infants. On the basis of videotaped interaction mothers were classified as 'abusive', 'neglecting', 'inept' or 'sensitive' – this grouping being found to correlate highly with the existing maltreatment classification, although none of those coding the observations were aware of the existing classifications. *Infant* patterns of interaction were classified as 'difficult', 'passive' or 'co-operative'. The findings are summarized in Table 7.1.

Of interest here is that mothers did not have to be highly skilled to get a 'co-operative' response; of further interest is that *some* infants remained co-operative despite abusive or neglectful responses from their mothers. Crittenden comments:

> These results supported a model of bidirectional
> effects between mother and infant, but one which
> appeared to be set in motion by the mother rather than
> the infant. Abused and neglected infants behaved in
> ways which could be expected to maintain their
> mothers' maltreating behaviour. (p. 92)

In an earlier pilot study by Crittenden 24 mothers identified as abusive and similarly rated on observed interaction were involved in an intervention study aimed at improving their interaction with their children, using video feedback and discussion. After four months of intervention the mothers were divided into two groups: those showing an improvement in sensitivity (16) and those who did not. Infant patterns of interaction were rated by separate coders for the same pre- and post-intervention tapes. In 10 of the 16 cases where the mother had increased in sensitivity,

Table 7.1 The relationship between maternal pattern of interaction and infant pattern of interaction (from Crittenden, 1985, p. 90, Table 1)

Maternal pattern of interaction	Infant pattern of interaction		
	Difficult	Passive	Co-operative
Abusive	<u>12</u>	1	4
Neglecting	3	<u>12</u>	5
Inept	4	3	<u>23</u>
Sensitive	1	1	<u>5</u>

Predicted association is indicated by underlining.

the infant showed the predicted increase in co-operation; this occurred in none of the infants whose mothers had shown no increase in sensitivity.

Crittenden concludes that this:

> [suggests] that infant behavior during interaction does not stem from an inherent temperamental trait which could be deemed to cause maltreatment. On the contrary, because changes in adult behavior were followed by changes in infant behavior, the results suggest that maltreated infants are resilient and capable of cooperative behavior. (p. 92)

In this study resilience (or invulnerability) was demonstrated in two ways:

1 Some abused or neglected infants remained co-operative;
2 Some infants became more co-operative when their mothers' sensitivity improved.

Cowen and Work (1988) reviewing the literature on resilience in children comment: 'Invulnerable children may ... hold a key that can productively turn mental health's present disproportional emphasis on pathology and its undoing, to a psychology of health and wellness' (p. 597). This claim sounds like that hardy perennial, North American optimism, but the point is none the less an important one.

The need is not for some simple minded shift from 'risk' factors to 'protective' factors. Characteristics of parents and children operate in interaction or *transaction*: abusive parents are more likely to make infants and children unco-operative; unco-operative children are more likely to call forth an abusive response. Protection from these effects is in the process of how the 'risk' is dealt with. Rutter (1987) in a sophisticated review of this issue (strongly recommended for further reading) comments: 'protection ... resides, not in the evasion of risk, but in successful engagement with it' (p. 318), and 'interaction effects are crucial for protective processes' (p. 319).

Rutter reviews the operation of these processes in relation to the differential effects of marital discord on boys as opposed to girls. Marital discord is frequently noted as a high frequency factor in child abuse cases (e.g. Creighton, 1992, p. 70). Rutter points to data from his own study (Rutter and Quinton, 1984) (Figure 7.1).

The histogram clearly shows that the increase in initial and persistent disturbance is much greater for boys than girls in families where there is marital disharmony (the data are from a

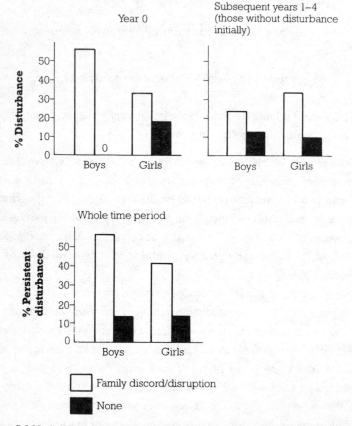

Figure 7.1 Marital discord and disturbance in children (cited in Rutter, 1987, p. 320, Figure 1. © American Orthopsychiatric Association, Inc. Reproduced with permission).

four-year longitudinal study of children with mentally ill parents). Rutter suggests a number of reasons:

- male vulnerability to psychosocial hazards, biologically determined;
- parents are more likely to quarrel in front of boys than girls;
- in a marital break-up, sons are more likely to be placed in care than daughters;
- boys are more likely to react with oppositional behaviour, which often leads to a negative response;
- boys are treated more punitively than girls, particularly for aggressive behaviour.

He concludes that:

> it may be inferred that the protection afforded by being female is in part a result of a lesser exposure to the risk factor, a reduced exposure that is a consequence of the immediate family context, the chain of interactions that follows, and the sequelae of family breakdown. (p. 320)

We are partly determined by what happens to us: but the effects of those external factors are filtered by our understanding in relation to ourselves. As Rutter points out in his discussion (p. 327) a wide variety of evidence attests to the importance of people's concepts of themselves, and their ability to deal with life's challenges. Two types of experience are crucial:

1 Secure and harmonious love relationships (and as has been seen, this need is manifest at an early age);
2 Successful accomplishment of tasks important to individuals (and we have seen that abuse affects competence and persistence adversely).

This summary reduction may appear to make the matter too simple. As we shall see in the final chapter dealing with prevention, it is anything but that.

8
THE PREVENTION OF ABUSE

The public health model of different levels of prevention – primary (before it happens), secondary (early treatment) and tertiary (minimizing effects) – has been around so long that it has become something of a cliché. As Gordon (1983) points out it has the attraction of being extremely simple. And it works best in dealing with health problems such as infectious disease where *causes*, numbers of *cases*, and the effectiveness of *treatments* can be clearly described and demonstrated.

Giovannoni (1982) comments: 'When it comes to social problems – those enmeshed in the complexities of social relationships – the translation of the usual models of preventive action poses serious conceptual and practical problems' (p. 23).

Two things are essential for the public health model of prevention to work in practice:

- clarity of *definition* of the problem to be prevented;
- knowledge of the *causes* of the problem.

We do not have that degree of clarity and certainty. Indeed, as the review of *fatal* child abuse in Chapter 4 demonstrated, we are far from being clear as to the scale and causes of the most extreme effects of physical abuse. In the discussion and review that follow, these points must be borne in mind.

Reviewing the literature on research and practice it is clear that primary prevention hardly exists, certainly at a level where it is, or could be, evaluated. The renaming of Child *Abuse* Registers as Child *Protection* Registers is more of a change of philosophy than a change in practice. Child-protection services are hard-pressed to deal with those cases that are referred to them after the event. In the UK the major part of Social Work/Social Services Departments' budgets is spent on child protection. Social workers work hard, and often imaginatively, to attempt to reduce the risk of further abuse but are limited in the scale of what they can do by their case-load. Nor is this work evaluated in any systematic fashion. Creighton (1993) points out that there is a lack of UK research on *re-abuse*: one common sense criterion of intervention effectiveness. A conservative US estimate is that re-abuse occurs in at least half of all cases referred to child-protection agencies (Magura, 1981).

It does seem, however, that systems of child protection (and public knowledge of these) have some regulating effect. Creighton (1985) points to the decrease in severe physical abuse in the NSPCC sample following the institution of Child Abuse Registers in 1974. But she also points to an upward trend again from the early 1980s, at least, as world economic conditions worsened.

Correlates are not necessarily *causes*, although they may point to 'probables'. The most consistent correlate of child abuse is poverty. Other correlates such as: single-parent status, teenage pregnancy and unemployment, whilst all probably adding their own distinctive component, seem to be mainly indices of poverty. Gelles (1989) found that, at least for women, who are usually the lone parent, it was being poor, not being single, that predisposed them to abuse. And reviewing the literature on young maternal age, Holden, Willis and Corcoran (1992) report:

> Young maternal age as a predictor of subsequent child
> maltreatment was evaluated in 10 separate
> investigations with mixed results. Six of the studies
> which did not support age as a risk factor were

generally well-controlled prospective investigations
... Those four studies which found younger mothers to
be at greater risk for subsequent child maltreatment
utilized retrospective designs. .... In addition, two of
these four investigations ... did not control for
socioeconomic status. When researchers controlled for
SES in the previously cited prospective investigations,
age no longer surfaced as an important predictive
variable. A similar pattern of results across
investigations was obtained for single marital status
during pregnancy. (p. 25)

This does *not* mean that we disregard maternal age or single-parent status (or unemployment or marital disharmony – Creighton, 1992) as indices of risk: rather that they should not be seen as fundamental or *causal*.

Criticizing the primary/secondary/tertiary prevention model, Gordon (1983) suggests that we should think in terms of *universal* measures (desirable for everybody); *selective* measures (for high-risk groups); and *indicated* measures (for identified groups or individuals) – the whole to be judged in terms of cost-benefit analysis.

Because child abuse is embedded in large-scale social problems endemic in our society, child abuse is endemic. But the maltreatment of children is not the only evil: poverty and unemployment have other effects, universally undesirable, as the literature on abuse and unemployment attests (e.g. Steinberg, Catalano and Dooley, 1981).

Most poor and unemployed parents, lone parents and teenage mothers do not abuse their children; but their position, in socioeconomic terms, renders them susceptible to a range of stresses. All of the problems are large-scale and require large-scale political action. It also means that, as a society, we have to decide what our social priorities are. Are we prepared to allow single mothers to live in relative poverty? Are we prepared to prevent or terminate teenage pregnancies? The two questions are largely related, and the scale of the problem is enormous.

Describing the situation in the US Unger and Wandersman (1985) report:

> Over one million teenage women are becoming
> pregnant every year, approximately 600,000 carrying
> their pregnancies to term ... As many as 23% of the
> infants born to very young teenage mothers have low
> birth weights ... Many of the risks of adolescent
> pregnancy are *not* primarily due to the physiological
> and psychological immaturity of teenage mothers. (pp.
> 29–30)

Pregnancy in under-age schoolgirls in the UK is so commonplace in the 1990s as to be unremarkable. There are good reasons (apart from the risk of child abuse and neglect) why this should be prevented, but we are a long way from providing adequate advice and contraception services to young people.

One 'universal' approach that might be seen as preventative is to target school-age adolescents with sex education and childcare programmes. These have the virtues of face validity and cheapness and can be administered widely. Unfortunately there is no evidence that they make young people more sexually responsible or better at parenting. Wald and Cohen (1988) commenting on evaluative research of parenting programmes observe that:

> These studies indicate that education programs can
> have a short-term impact on the participants'
> knowledge and attitudes. Unfortunately, there is little
> reason to believe that the changes in knowledge or
> attitudes generated by education programs are likely
> to have much impact on physical abuse.
>
> Our pessimism derives from the limited success that
> even the most extensive education programs have had
> on behavior. (p. 310)

The lack of effect of social-education programmes has been widely demonstrated – for example, in relation to drug abuse (Davies and Coggans, 1991, p. 61) and child pedestrian behaviour (Thomson, 1991, p. 71). All the programmes have the characteristic of being 'face valid', but the faith in these 'knowledge enhancement' approaches represents a fundamental misconception of the determinants of human behaviour.

'SELECTIVE' INTERVENTION

Social improvements that affect everybody also help parents with the potential for physical abuse. They will not have been identified as such, nor is there need to do so in an ideal world. The nearest we get to it is when there are dramatic improvements in national economies: child abuse appears to worsen in times of economic recession.

'Selective' interventions involve identifying high-risk populations of parents *before* abuse occurs and providing forms of support which are predicted to reduce the likelihood. Even if we were sure as to what forms of intervention would work (and we are not) there are two insuperable problems attendant on such attempts:

1 Because the number of parents who will abuse their children during their lifetime is a small proportion of all parents, accurate prediction is impossible. With a *population base rate* of around 5 per cent, even with good predictors (which we do not have) two things happen:

- some parents who will abuse are not identified (false negatives);
- a *very* large number of parents who will *not* abuse are identified (false positives).

It is this last group that present the major problem because they would absorb resources unnecessarily.

2 Identifying people as 'potential abusers' is seen as stigmatic and an infringement of human rights.

A compromise is to identify groups of parents, particularly mothers, who are significantly at risk (young, single, poor, with children under two) but who demonstrably need support on simple humane grounds; as, to some extent, do all mothers with very young children.

There are a number of reasons why such a selective emphasis should focus on parents with very young children. We know that the most severe forms of physical abuse occur in the under-two age-range. It is also known that the mothers of such children are particularly vulnerable in mental health terms (Brown and Harris, 1978).

A major strand in the literature on the abuse of young children both theoretical and empirical, is concerned with the role of *attachment*: the mutual pleasure and security that the mother and child derive from each other. Note that this is not just a matter of the mother being 'attached' to the child: it is an interactive process and is not complete until the middle of the first year of life when the child shows clear evidence of recognition and preference for the mother. In attachment theory the absence of this bond means that the inhibitors that usually prevent maltreatment are not in place. This could partly explain the peculiar vulnerability of young babies to abuse.

Crittenden and Ainsworth (1989) argue that anxious/insecure attachment is a critical concept in the aetiology of maltreatment and that patterns of attachment behaviour affect the subsequent course of a child's development. They suggest that insecure-attachment relationships, apart from being mutually unsatisfactory, render all members of a family more vulnerable to external stresses such as poverty and unemployment, and affect the ability to maintain stable relationships.

Intervention that improves the quality of the relationship between a mother and her young child would seem a high priority, particularly if it is in the context of improved *social support.*

Belsky (1984) suggests that social support works in three main ways:

- by providing *emotional* support;
- by providing *practical* help;
- by reinforcing *social expectations* of 'good' parenting.

This is most satisfactorily (and economically) provided by the immediate family and local community but a consistent finding is that *professional* support has positive effects on high-risk, young single parents. Some of these studies will now be considered in detail because of their practical implications.

SELECTIVE SUPPORT: EMPIRICAL STUDIES INVOLVING MOTHERS AND YOUNG CHILDREN

Gray *et al.* (1977) were the first to carry out a well-designed controlled intervention study. They identified 100 high-risk mothers prenatally and randomly assigned them to either an intervention or a control group. Intervention started at birth, involving greater contact with professional workers in hospital and community and weekly home-visiting by a nurse. At follow-up, between 17 and 35 months after the birth, significant differences were found with only moderate maltreatment episodes in the intervention group whereas five children in the control group had been hospitalized because of injuries. A further study by the same authors (1979), where several hundred high-risk families received nurse home-visiting for 18 months, found no serious injuries in the children.

Crockenburg (1981) compared two groups of young mothers aged from 17 to 19, one group in England, one in the US. The English group received regular, professional support from home-visiting nurses; the US group received no professional help. Most noticeably the mothers in the English group were more positive in their behaviour towards their babies and engaged in a more responsive way, smiling at them more, for example.

The most sophisticated research into the effects of regular home-visiting by nurses is that of Olds and his associates (Olds *et al.*, 1986). In the US 400 women were enrolled in the study prior to the birth of their first baby if they had any one of three 'risk' characteristics:

- age under 19
- single-parent
- low socioeconomic status.

Of the sample 23 per cent possessed all three characteristics. Mothers were randomly assigned to one of four treatment conditions:

1 A control group that participated only in data collection before and after;
2 A group that only received transport for medical appointments;
3 A group that received extensive *pre*natal nurse home-visiting and transport for subsequent medical appointments;
4 A group that received extensive nurse home-visiting *post*natally as well as the services provided to group 3.

The authors found that for the mothers at greatest risk (teenage *and* single *and* poor) the effect of nurse-visiting was greatest: 19 per cent of the mothers in the control group had abused or neglected their children in the first two years of life as against 4 per cent in the nurse-visited group. The authors observe:

> Although the treatment contrasts for the groups at
> lower risk did not reach statistical significance,
> virtually all of the contrasts were in the expected
> directions. Moreover, in the comparison condition the

incidence of abuse and neglect increased as the
number of risk factors accumulated, but in the nurse-
visited condition, the incidence of abuse and neglect
remained relatively low, even in those groups at
higher risk. Also, the incidence of maltreatment in
treatment 3 (nurse-visited: pregnancy) in general, was
between the infancy nurse-visited and comparison
conditions. (p. 71)

They go on to make the following interesting comment:

The nurse-visited women reported less crying and
fussiness on the part of their babies. Because reports of
temperament and behavioral problems may be just as
much a reflection of the mother's characteristics as the
child's, we interpret reports of excessive crying and
irritability as a problem in the parent-child
relationship. (p. 76)

The high abuse rates in children under three is likely to be due to
the specially stressful character of parenting at this stage and
because young parents are less well-equipped to cope. But it is
also the stage when children are least 'visible'. One function of
regular professional visiting is to increase 'visibility'.

Once children reach nursery age (three plus) and as nursery
provision increases (and it is often differentially allocated to
socially disadvantaged children in the state sector in the UK) they
become subject to daily scrutiny by teachers and nurses. The
detection of suspicious bruising and other injuries is part of the
regular training of such professionals and there are statutory
procedures for notification. This vigilance, and parental knowledge of it, may also act as a form of preventive social control.
Nurseries and schools also provide parents with relief from the
continuous care of children.

There is good reason to believe (Oliver, 1983) that much abuse
is concentrated in a number of problem families in well-defined

areas, usually housing estates (Cotterill, 1988). Although prevention of further abuse may be difficult, and more research on re-abuse is necessary, social workers do come to know these families well and so 'manage' the problems. But the continuing demands mean that, at this stage, professional involvement is not really preventive. Current research by the author (Gillham and Tanner, 1993) shows that 30 per cent of cases of physical abuse registered in 1991 in the Strathclyde Region of Scotland had been previously registered. The chronic character of these problems underlines the need for large-scale social improvements and high-quality primary prevention targeted on *all* parents of very young children. But especially those who are young themselves, single, poor and with a history of abuse in their own childhood.

Once established, abusive patterns of interaction can be self-maintaining: as we have seen in the review of the effects of abusive parenting styles on very young children. But abusive parenting exists in, and is subject to modification by, the current ethos regarding the rights of adults to punish children physically. As noted in Chapter 4, Garbarino (1977) suggests that society's sanctioning of the physical punishment of children is one of the necessary preconditions of abuse. The severe physical punishment of children in schools, with the cane and the strap, was general in the UK twenty years ago and was not abolished in state-funded schools until 1987 (Leach, 1993). What this means is that the abusive treatment of children is in a continual process of redefinition. What is permissible in the wider society at any one time is the standard against which individual parents' treatment of their children is measured and judged and, to some extent, by which they judge themselves.

REFERENCES

Asterisked (*) references are recommended for further reading.

Aber, J.L. and Cicchetti, D. (1984) The socio-emotional development of maltreated children: An empirical and theoretical analysis. In H.E. Fitzgerald, B.M. Lester and M.W. Yogman (eds), *Theory and Research in Behavioral Pediatrics* (Volume 2). New York: Plenum Press.

Alfaro, J.D. (1991) What can we learn from child abuse fatalities? A synthesis of nine studies. In D.J. Besharov (ed.), *Protecting Children from Abuse and Neglect*. Springfield, IL: Charles C. Thomas.

Altman, D.H. and Smith, R.L. (1960) Unrecognized trauma in infants and children. *Journal of Bone and Joint Surgery*, **42a**, 407–13.

Anderson, R., Ambrosino, R., Valentine, D. and Lauderdale, M. (1983) Child deaths attributed to abuse and neglect: An empirical study. *Children and Youth Services Review*, **5**, 75–89.

Astley, R. (1953) Multiple metaphyseal fractures. *British Journal of Radiology*, **26**, 577.

*Baker, A.W. and Duncan, S.P (1985) Child sexual abuse: A study of prevalence in Great Britain. *Child Abuse and Neglect*, **9**(4), 457–67.

Baldwin, J.A. and Oliver, J.E. (1975) Epidemiology and family characteristics of severely-abused children. *British Journal of Preventive and Social Medicine*, **29**, 205–21.

*Belsky, J. (1980) Child maltreatment: An ecological integration. *American Psychologist*, **35**, 320–35.

References

Belsky, J. (1984) The determinants of parenting: A processes model. *Child Development*, **55**, 83–96.

Berger, D. (1979) Child abuse simulating 'near-miss' sudden infant death syndrome. *The Journal of Pediatrics*, **95**, 554–6.

Bronfenbrenner, U. (1977) Toward an experimental ecology of human development. *American Psychologist*, **32**, 513–31.

Brown, C. (1992) Foreword to: S.J. Creighton, *Child Abuse Trends in England and Wales 1988–1990*. London: NSPCC.

Brown, G.W. and Harris, T. (1978) *Social Origins of Depression: A Study of Psychiatric Disorder in Women*. London: Tavistock.

Bureau of the Census (1985) *Statistical Abstract of the United States, 1985*. Washington, DC: US Government Printing Office.

Butler, N.R. and Golding, J. (eds) (1986) *From Birth to Five: A Study of Health and Behaviour of Britain's Five Year Olds*. Oxford: Pergamon.

Caffey, J. (1946) Multiple fractures in long bones of infants suffering from chronic subdural hematoma. *American Journal of Roentgenology*, **56**, 163–73.

Caffey, J. (1957) Some traumatic lesions in growing bones other than fractures and dislocations: Clinical and radiological features. *British Journal of Radiology*, **30**, 225–38.

Caplan, G. (1974) *Support Systems and Community Mental Health*. New York: Behavioral Publications.

Cattell, R.B. (1965) *The Scientific Analysis of Personality*. Harmondsworth: Penguin.

Cicchetti, D. and Rizley, R. (1981) Developmental perspectives on the etiology, intergenerational transmission, and sequelae of child maltreatment. *New Directions for Child Maltreatment*, **11**, 31–55.

Cotterill, A.M. (1988) The geographic distribution of child abuse in an inner city borough. *Child Abuse and Neglect*, 12, 461–7.

Cowen, E.L. and Work, W.C. (1988) Resilient children, psychological wellness and primary prevention. *American Journal of Community Psychology*, 16, 591–607.

*Creighton, S.J. (1985) An epidemiological study of abused children and their families in the United Kingdom between 1977 and 1982. *Child Abuse and Neglect*, 9, 441–8.

*Creighton, S.J. (1992) *Child Abuse Trends in England and Wales 1988–1990*. London: NSPCC.

Creighton, S.J. (1993) Personal communication.

*Creighton, S.J. and Noyes, P. (1989) *Child Abuse Trends in England and Wales 1983–1987*. London: NSPCC.

Crittenden, P.M. (1985) Maltreated infants: Vulnerability and resilience. *Journal of Child Psychology and Psychiatry*, 26(1), 85–96.

*Crittenden, P.M. and Ainsworth, M.D.S. (1989) Child maltreatment and attachment theory. In D. Cicchetti and V. Carlson (eds), *Child Maltreatment*. New York: Cambridge University Press.

Crockenburg, S. (1981) Professional support and care of infants by adolescent mothers in England and the United States. *Journal of Pediatric Psychology*, 10, 413–28.

Davies, J. and Coggans, N. (1991) *The Facts About Adolescent Drug Abuse*. London: Cassell.

Department of Health (1990) *Children and Young Persons on Child Protection Registers Year Ending 31 March 1989 England*. London: Government Statistical Service.

Department of Health (1991a) *Child Abuse: A Study of Inquiry Reports 1980–1989*. London: HMSO.

References

Department of Health (1991b) *Children and Young Persons on Child Protection Registers Year Ending 31 March 1990 England.* London: Government Statistical Service.

Department of Health (1992) *Children and Young Persons on Child Protection Registers Year Ending 31 March 1991 England.* London: Government Statistical Services.

Department of Health and Social Security (1973) *The Report of the Committee of Inquiry into the Care and Supervision Provided in Relation to Maria Colwell.* London: HMSO.

Department of Health and Social Security (1974) Non-accidental injury to children. LASSL, (74) 13.

Department of Health and Social Security (1982) *Child Abuse: A Study of Inquiry Reports 1973–1981.* London: HMSO.

Department of Health and Social Security (1988) *Working Together.* London: HMSO.

Douglas, J. (1989) *Behaviour Problems in Young Children.* London: Routledge.

Elmer, E. and Gregg, G. (1967) Developmental characteristics of abused children. *Pediatrics*, **40**, 596–602.

Emans, S.J., Woods, E.R., Flagg, N.T. and Freeman, A. (1987) Genital findings in sexually abused, symptomatic and asymptomatic girls. *Pediatrics*, **79**, 778–85.

*Emery, J.L. (1985) Infanticide, filicide and cot death. *Archives of Disease in Childhood*, **60**, 505–7.

Emery, J.L. (1986) Letter. *New England Journal of Medicine*, **315**, 1676.

Farber, E.A. and Egeland, B. (1987) Invulnerability among abused and neglected children. In E.J. Anthony and B.J. Cohler (eds), *The Invulnerable Child.* New York: Guilford Press.

Fedrick, J. (1973) Sudden infant deaths in the Oxford Record

Linkage Area: The mother. *British Journal of Preventive and Social Medicine*, **28**, 93–7.

Finkel, M.A. (1989) Child sexual abuse: A physician's introduction to historical and medical validation. *Journal of the American Osteopathic Association*, **89**(3), 1143–9.

Finkelhor, D. (1979) *Sexually Victimized Children*. New York: Free Press.

Finkelhor, D. (1987) The sexual abuse of children: Current research reviewed. *Psychiatric Annals*, **17**(4), 233–41.

Finkelhor, D. and Hotaling, G.T. (1984) Sexual abuse in the National Incidence Study of Child Abuse and Neglect: An appraisal. *Child Abuse and Neglect*, **8**, 23–33.

Fisher, S.H. (1958) Skeletal manifestations of parent-induced trauma in infants and children. *Southern Medical Journal*, **51**, 956–60.

Fontana, V.J. (1971) *The Maltreated Child* (2nd edition). Springfield, IL: Charles C. Thomas.

Frodi, A.M., Lamb, M.E., Leavitt, L., Donovan, W., Neff, C. and Sherry, D. (1978) Fathers' and mothers' responses to infant smiles and cries. *Infant Behavior and Development*, **1**, 187–98.

Garbarino, J. (1976) A preliminary study of some ecological correlates of child abuse: The impact of socioeconomic stress on mothers. *Child Development*, **47**, 178–85.

*Garbarino, J. (1977) The human ecology of child maltreatment: A conceptual model for research. *Journal of Marriage and the Family*, **39**, 721–7.

Garbarino, J. and Crouter, A. (1978) Defining the community context for parent-child relations: The correlates of child maltreatment. *Child Development*, **49**, 604–16.

Garbarino, J. and Sherman, D. (1980) High-risk neighbourhoods and high-risk families: The human ecology of child maltreatment. *Child Development,* **51**, 188–98.

Garfinkel, I. and McLanahan, S.S. (1986) *Single Mothers and Their Children: A New American Dilemma.* Washington, DC: The Urban Institute.

*Gelardo, M.S. and Sanford, E.E. (1987) Child abuse and neglect: A review of the literature. *School Psychology Review,* **16**(2), 137–55.

Gelles, R.J. (1989) Child abuse and violence in single-parent families: Parent absence and economic deprivation. *American Journal of Orthopsychiatry,* **59**(4), 492–501.

George, C. and Main, M. (1979) Social interactions of young abused children: Approach, avoidance and aggression. *Child Development,* **49**, 306–18.

Gibson, A., Brooke, H. and Keeling, J. (1991) Reduction in sudden infant death syndrome in Scotland. *The Lancet,* **338**, 1595.

Gil, D. (1970) *Violence Against Children: Physical Child Abuse in the United States.* Cambridge: Harvard University Press.

*Gillham, B. (1991) *The Facts About Child Sexual Abuse.* London: Cassell.

Gillham, B. (1992) Evidence in cases of child sexual abuse. *Journal of the Law Society of Scotland,* **37**(6), 225–8.

Gillham, B. and Tanner, G. (1993) *Unpublished research data.* Glasgow: Department of Psychology, University of Strathclyde.

Giovannoni, J. (1982) Prevention of child abuse and neglect: Research and policy issues. *Social Work Research and Abstracts,* **18**, 23–31.

Gordon, R.S. (1983) An operational classification of disease prevention. *Public Health Reports,* **98**, 107–9.

Gray, J.D., Cutler, C.A., Dean, J.G. and Kempe, C.H. (1977) Prediction and prevention of child abuse and neglect. *Child Abuse and Neglect*, 1, 45–58.

Gray, J.D., Cutler, C.A., Dean, J.G. and Kempe, C.H. (1979) Prediction and prevention of child abuse and neglect. *Journal of Social Issues*, 35, 127–39.

Green, A.H., Gaines, R.W. and Sandgrund, A. (1974) Child abuse: Pathological syndrome of family interaction. *American Journal of Psychiatry*, 131, 882–6.

Groth, A.N., Burgess, A.W., Birnbaum, H.J. and Gary, T.S. (1978) A study of the child molester: Myths and realities. *Journal of the American Criminal Justice Association*, 41, 17–22.

Gwinn, J.L., Lewin, K.W. and Peterson, H.G. (1961) Roentgenographic manifestations of unsuspected trauma in infancy. *Journal of the American Medical Association*, 176, 926–9.

Herrenkohl, R.C. and Herrenkohl, E.C. (1981) Some antecedents and developmental consequences of child maltreatment. *New Directions for Child Development*, 11, 57–76.

Hobbs, C.J. and Wynne, J.M. (1987) Child sexual abuse: An increasing rate of diagnosis. *Lancet*, 2, 837–41.

Hobbs, C.J. and Wynne, J.M. (1990) The sexually abused battered child. *Archives of Disease in Childhood*, 65(4), 423–7.

*Holden, E.W., Willis, D.J. and Corcoran, M.M (1992) Preventing child maltreatment during the prenatal/perinatal period. In *Prevention of Child Maltreatment: Developmental and Ecological Perspectives*. New York: John Wiley.

Home Office (1990) *Criminal Statistics England and Wales 1989.* London: HMSO.

*Howitt, D. (1992) *Child Abuse Errors.* London: Harvester Wheatsheaf.

Hunter, R. and Kilstrom, N. (1979) Breaking the cycle of abusive families. *American Journal of Psychiatry*, **136**, 1320–2.

Hunter, R.S., Kilstrom, N., Kraybill, E.N. and Loda, F. (1978) Antecedents of child neglect and abuse in premature infants: A prospective study in a newborn intensive care unit. *Pediatrics*, **61**, 629–35.

Jason, J. and Andereck, N.D. (1983) Fatal child abuse in Georgia: The epidemiology of severe physical child abuse. *Child Abuse and Neglect*, **7**, 1–9.

Jason, J., Carpenter, M.M. and Tyler, C.W. (1983) Under-recording of infant homicide in the United States. *American Journal of Public Health*, **73**(2), 195–7.

Jason, J., Williams, S.L., Burton, A. and Rochat, R. (1982) Epidemiologic differences between sexual and physical child abuse. *Journal of the American Medical Association*, **247**(24), 3344–8.

Johnson, B. and Morse, H. (1968) *The Battered Child: A Study of Children with Inflicted Injuries*. Denver, CO: Denver Department of Welfare.

Kadushin, A. and Martin, J.A. (1981) *Child Abuse: An Inter-actional Event*. New York: Columbia University Press.

Kagan, J. (1971) *Change and Continuity in Infancy*. New York: John Wiley.

Kaufman, J. and Zigler, E. (1987) Do abused children become abusive parents? *American Journal of Orthopsychiatry*, **57**(2), 186–92.

*Kaufman, J. and Zigler, E. (1992) The prevention of child maltreatment: Programming, research and policy. In D.J. Willis, E.W. Holden and M. Rosenberg (eds), *Prevention of Child Maltreatment: Developmental and Ecological Perspectives*. New York: John Wiley.

Kempe, C.H. and Helfer, R.E. (1980) *The Battered Child* (3rd edition). Chicago: Chicago University Press.

*Kempe, C.H., Silverman, F.N., Steele, B.F., Droegemuller, W. and Silver, H.K. (1962) The battered-child syndrome. *Journal of the American Medical Association,* **181**(1), 17–24.

*Leach, P. (1993) Should parents hit their children? *The Psychologist,* **6**(5), 216–20.

Lewis, J., Samuels, M. and Southall, D. (1993) Is the decline in cot deaths due to child-health reorganisation? *The Lancet,* **341**, 51.

McCann, J., Voris, J., Simon, M. and Wells, R. (1989) Perianal findings in prepubertal children selected for nonabuse: A descriptive study. *Child Abuse and Neglect,* **13**, 179–93.

Magura, M. (1981) Are services to protect children effective? *Children and Youth Services Review,* **3**, 193.

Margolin, L. (1990) Fatal child neglect. *Child Welfare,* **69**(4), 309–19.

Martin, H.P. and Beezley, P. (1977) Behavioral observations of abused children. *Developmental Medicine and Child Neurology,* **19**, 373–87.

Meadow, R. (1984) Fictitious epilepsy. *The Lancet,* **ii**, 25–8.

Miller, D.S. (1959) Fractures among children. *Minnesota Medicine,* **42**, 1209–13 and 1414–25.

Miller, S.H. (1984) The relationship between adolescent childbearing and child maltreatment. *Child Welfare,* **63**(6), 553–7.

Mischel, W. (1968) *Personality and Assessment.* New York: John Wiley.

Mitchel, L.B. (1989) Report on fatalities from NCPCA. *Protecting Children,* **6**, 3–5.

References

Mrazek, P.M. and Bentovim, A. (1981) Recognition of child sexual abuse in the United Kingdom. In P.M. Mrazek, M. Lynch, A. Bentovim, P.B. Mrazek and C.H. Kempe (eds), *Sexually Abused Children and Their Families.* Oxford: Pergamon.

Newberger, E.H., Reed, R.B., Daniel, J.H., Hyde, J.N. and Kotelchuik, M. (1977) Pediatric social illness: Etiology classification. *Pediatrics,* **60,** 178–85.

Newlands, M. and Emery, J.S. (1991) Child abuse and cot deaths. *Child Abuse and Neglect,* **15,** 275–8.

Office of Population Censuses and Surveys (1989) *Birth Statistics.* London: HMSO.

Office of Population Censuses and Surveys (1991a) *General Household Survey 1989.* London: HMSO.

Office of Population Censuses and Surveys (1991b) *Mortality Statistics: Childhood 1988.* London: HMSO.

Office of Population Censuses and Surveys (1992a) *General Household Survey 1990.* London: HMSO.

Office of Population Censuses and Surveys (1992b) *Mortality Statistics: Perinatal and Infant: Social and Biological Factors.* London: HMSO.

*****Olds, D.L., Henderson, C.R., Chamberlin, R. and Tatelbaum, R.** (1986) Preventing child abuse and neglect: A randomized trial of nurse home visitation. *Pediatrics,* **78**(1), 65–78.

Oliver, J.E. (1983) Dead children from problem families in N.E. Wiltshire. *British Medical Journal,* **286,** 115–17.

O'Toole, R., Turbett, P. and Nalepka, C. (1983) Theories, professional knowledge and diagnosis of child abuse. In D. Finkelhor, R.J. Gelles, G.T. Hotaling and M.A. Straus (eds), *The Dark Side of Families.* Beverley Hills: Sage.

*Pelton, L.H. (1978) Child abuse and neglect: The myth of classlessness. *American Journal of Orthopsychiatry*, **48**, 608–17.

Pervin, L.A. (1978) *Current Controversies and Issues in Personality*. New York: John Wiley.

Pinchbeck, I. and Hewitt, M. (1973) *Children in English Society* (Volume II). London: Routledge and Kegan Paul.

Pritchard, C. (1992) Children's homicide as an indicator of effective child protection: A comparative study of Western European statistics. *British Journal of Social Work*, **22**(6), 663–84.

*Radbill, S.X. (1968) A history of child abuse and infanticide. In R.E. Helfer and C.H. Kempe (eds), *The Battered Child*. Chicago: The University of Chicago Press.

Registrar General Scotland (1992) *Annual Report 1991*. Edinburgh: General Register Office.

Reidy, T. (1977) The aggressive characteristics of abused and neglected children. *Journal of Clinical Psychology*, **33**, 1140–5.

Roberts, J., Lynch, M.A. and Golding, J. (1980) Postneonatal mortality in children from abusing families. *British Medical Journal*, **281**, 102–4.

Rosen, C.L., Frost, J.D. Jr., Bricker, T., Tarnow, J.D., Gillette, P.C. and Dunlavy, S. (1983) Two siblings with recurrent cardiorespiratory arrest: Munchausen syndrome by proxy or child abuse? *Pediatrics*, **71**, 715–20.

Rosenthal, J.A. (1988) Patterns of reported child abuse and neglect. *Child Abuse and Neglect*, **12**, 263–71.

*Russell, A.B. and Trainor, C.M. (1984) *Trends in Child Abuse and Neglect: A National Perspective*. Denver: The American Humane Association.

*Rutter, M. (1987) Psychosocial resilience and protective mechanisms. *American Journal of Orthopsychiatry*, **57**(3), 316–31.

References

Rutter, M. and Quinton, D. (1984) Long-term follow-up of women institutionalized in childhood: Factors promoting good functioning in adult life. *British Journal of Developmental Psychology*, **18**, 225–34.

Seagull, E.A.W. (1987) Social support and child maltreatment: A review of the evidence. *Child Abuse and Neglect*, **11**, 41–52.

Silverman, F. (1953) Roentgen manifestations of unrecognized skeletal trauma in infants. *American Journal of Roentgenology*, **69**, 413–26.

Skinner, A.E. and Castle, R.L. (1969) *78 Battered Children: A Retrospective Study*. London: NSPCC.

Southall, D.P., Stebbens, V.A., Rees, S.V., Lang, M.H., Warner, J.O. and Shinebourne, E.A. (1987) Apnoeic episodes induced by smothering: Two cases identified by covert video surveillance. *British Medical Journal*, **294**, 1637–41.

Starr, R.H. (ed.) (1982) *Child Abuse Prediction: Policy Implications*. Cambridge, MA: Bollinger.

Steinberg, L.D., Catalano, R. and Dooley, D. (1981) Economic antecedents of child abuse and neglect. *Child Development*, **52**, 975–85.

Straus, M.A. (1979) Family patterns and child abuse in a nationally representative American sample. *Child Abuse and Neglect*, **3**, 213–25.

*Straus, M.A. and Gelles, R.J. (1986) Societal change and change in family violence from 1975 to 1985 as revealed by two national surveys. *Journal of Marriage and the Family*, **48**, 465–79.

Straus, M.A., Gelles, R.J. and Steinmetz, S.K. (1980) *Behind Closed Doors: Violence in the American Family*. Garden City, NY: Doubleday, Anchor Press.

Thomson, J. (1991) *The Facts About Child Pedestrian Accidents*. London: Cassell.

Tinbergen, N. (1951) *The Study of Instinct*. London: Oxford University Press.

Unger, D.G. and Wandersman, L.P. (1985) Social support and adolescent mothers: Action research contributions to theory and application. *Journal of Social Issues*, **41**(1), 29–45.

Vernon, P.E. (1964) *Personality Assessment: A Critical Survey*. London: Methuen.

Wald, M.S. and Cohen, S. (1988) Preventing child abuse – what will it take? In D.J. Besharov (ed.), *Protecting Children from Abuse and Neglect*. Springfield, IL: Charles C. Thomas.

Wasz-Hockert, O., Michelsson, K. and Lind, O. (1985) Twenty-five years of Scandinavian research. In M. Lester and C.F.Z. Boukydis (eds), *Infant Crying: Theoretical and Research Perspectives*. New York: Plenum.

Wilson, A.L. (1990) The State of South Dakota's child: 1989. *South Dakota Journal of Medicine*, **43**(1), 5–10.

Woolley, P.V. and Evans, W.A. (1955) Significance of skeletal lesions in infants resembling those of traumatic origin. *Journal of the American Medical Association*, **158**, 539–43.

Zumwalt, R.E. and Hirsch, C.S. (1980) Subtle fatal child abuse. *Human Pathology*, **11**, 167–74.

INDEX